The Other Side of Power

The Other Side of Power

CLAUDE M. STEINER

Grove Press, Inc./New York

First Hardcover Edition 1981
First Printing 1981
ISBN: 0-394-51950-7
Library of Congress Catalog Card Number: 80-8921

First Evergreen Edition 1981
First Printing 1981
ISBN: 0-394-17926-9
Library of Congress Catalog Card Number: 80-8921

Library of Congress Cataloging in Publication Data

Steiner, Claude, 1935-
    The other side of power.
    Bibliography: p.254
    1. Control (Psychology) I. Title. [DNLM: 1. Inter-
personal relations   2. Volition.   BF 632 S8220]
BF611.S72 1981   158   80-8921
ISBN 0-394-51950-7   AACR2
ISBN 0-394-17926-9 (pbk.)

Manufactured in the United States of America

GROVE PRESS, INC., 196 West Houston Street, New York, N.Y. 10014

To the female influences in my life, in particular to

Gaiea

Valerie

Hedi

Ursula

Mimi

Hogie

Carmen

Becky

Melissa

Darca

Denali

Diana

Acknowledgments

This book is the sequel to *Scripts People Live*. Consequently, I must thank, first of all, all those who contributed to that book: in particular Eric Berne, my teacher, and the early members of the Radical Psychiatry movement, especially Becky Jenkins, Joy Marcus, Bob Schwebel, and Hogie Wyckoff, with whom I developed my first ideas about power and power abuse.

Since I started work on this book, almost ten years ago, I have had the good fortune to discuss the other side of power with hundreds of people at lectures and workshops, and at after-dinner discussions with students, friends, and colleagues. Every one of these exchanges added to my understanding of the subject and I want to thank those many people whose interest and comments helped me shape the ideas herein.

I also want to thank (in the approximate order of their reading) Carmen Kerr, Fred Jordan, Anodea Judith, Robert Schwebel, Charlotte Sheedy, Katherine Williams, Bruce Carroll, Melanie Jenkins, Hogie Wyckoff, Ron LeVaco, Melissa Farley, Jayme Canton, Karen McNeil, Alan Rinzler, Ruth Capers, and Barney Rosset for their careful review and useful comments about the book at various stages of its completion.

Special thanks are due to Mimi Steiner and Caryn Levine, both of whose feedback substantially affected the final form of the book. Caryn, in particular, provided constant comments as she typed draft after draft, and her imprint upon the final product is all-pervasive. I cannot thank her enough for her part in this book.

The members of the Radical Psychiatry Collective, of which I am a member, have, with their constructive criticism and support, made a deep impression upon my thinking about power. I thank Hogie Wyckoff, Becky Jenkins, Robert Schwebel, Beth Roy, Mary Selkirk, Darca Nicholson, Jude La Barre, Shelby Morgan, and Jo Ann Costello for their participation in my life and work.

Finally I want to thank Kent Carroll for his many helpful suggestions and for the work of editing this book and guiding it to its final form.

CONTENTS

The Other Side of Power

INTRODUCTION

I have always been interested in power. When I was a kid, I built a water wheel which spun around and allowed me to fantasize machinery driven by my little engine.

I vividly remember how, as a fourteen-year-old, after months of work on a broken-down 125 C.C. Royal Enfield motorcycle, 1935 vintage, I finally got it fired up. Almost miraculously, it seemed, the engine started and I rode it down a crowded Mexico City street. The exhilaration of the pull which the small engine exerted on my arms and seat was as big a rush as I have ever felt. I became hooked on engines, gasoline, motorcycles, and cars and learned the macho driving style of Mexican bus drivers. Being propelled about by a bigger and bigger internal combustion power plant became my principal ambition in life.

In college I owned a souped-up 1938 Ford coupe. Compared to their four-cylinder predecessors, those Ford V–8 engines were a whole new breed of powerhouses. The sound of the thirsty machine sucking air and gasoline and the feel of its acceleration, after driving tame Dodges and Chevrolets, was as delicious as the sexual experiences I hungered after and never seemed to find. I felt weak, didn't like to walk, and feared sports. But having a car made me feel powerful.

Cars and money were intimately connected. More money meant more powerful wheels. My first real money was made as an auto mechanic while studying engineering

15

in Los Angeles in the middle 1950s. Everything in my environment conspired to keep me interested in horsepower. Plenty of cheap gas, millions of hot cars on the roads, car lots and junkyards. The in-crowd spent their leisure hours dragging between traffic lights. Horsepower was what everyone seemed to desire and Detroit delivered it. Back then, anyone who wanted it badly enough could get 300 horses (think of it, 300 horses!) under the hood of a stock Chrysler by walking to the nearest dealer.

Being involved with machinery and tools made me aware of the workings of physical force. How much tension was enough to loosen but not to strip a nut or a bolt. How much leverage was needed to move something heavy. How much pressure a piece of metal or wood could take without bending or splitting. Where and how to push and pull to achieve desired effects. I became a user of tools.

Cars and machinery appear in many examples in this book; probably because I had my first satisfying lessons about power while working with machines. Until then, my experiences had been largely about powerlessness. The early taste of power coming from using machines made a deep impression on me.

What I learned from machines turned out to be very useful, but it also created my tendency to think in mechanical metaphors. Machine thinking—logical, technical, rational, linear, scientific thinking—powerful as it may be, is also unable to speak to the realities of love, hate, hope, fear, joy or guilt.

Unfortunately, most of the world's power is held by men who would like to think only in the rational and scientific mode (though the thinking which guides their decisions is not even always scientific or rational). To them, whatever cannot be encompassed by rationality has no reality; therefore emotions are not to be considered real, important, or valid. Because I grew up thinking that way myself, I was emotionally illiterate for the first thirty-five years of my life. I was unable to account for and deal with my own or any one else's emotions and operated as if emotions did not exist. I tried to be precise and factual in all my decisions, but was actually driven by my emotions while I ignored the factual world of feelings.

In time I became dissatisfied with my mastery of mechanical things. I must have sensed that its scope was limited and that my needs for power would be better served by learning control over people, rather than machines. My interest, quite logically, turned to psychology. First I thought about hypnosis. I fantasized having people—especially women—under my hypnotic control. Then I became interested in psychotherapy. Being the Doctor, respected, listened to, loved by his patients, was an exciting day dream. I must also have been excited by the prospect of being able to use—from a position of power—all of the controlling maneuvers which had been used on me and other powerless people.

Of course, the controlling aspects of the profession weren't my only interest in it. There was another side of me; I also enjoyed the idea of being able to help people, being able to give effective and wise counsel, and taking pride in my craftsmanship. But the desire for control was unmistakable. In time, I obtained a doctorate in clinical psychology, developed a private practice, and obtained more powerful cars, more power tools, more money, and, eventually, even more women. My feelings of mastery and power continued to increase. I had control over myself, my destiny, my feelings, and I had control over other people. I had achieved the American Dream.

In time I found out that what I had achieved was not the American Dream, but the American Nightmare.

I found that I did not really control my feelings, but that they controlled me. Anger, guilt, fear, and envy affected me constantly. I wondered if my success and my feelings of self-determination were the result of luck, rather than real achievement. I came to realize that my control over others was tenuous at best and would eventually backfire. I eventually learned the fallacies upon which the American Dream was based—especially the belief that Control is power. What I learned prompted me to write this book.

Many people might benefit from reading *The Other Side of Power*. People who feel weak and are habitually being controlled and overpowered may want to learn how this is being done to them and how to avoid it. Some people who feel strong and are in the habit of controlling others may be uneasy or downright uncomfortable about the fact. They can learn how to stop abusing power without becoming powerless. Everyone can learn the many paths to power available to them, other than Control and manipulation of others.

We have much to lose from pursuing the conventional American power dream; it can no longer bring us what we want. The odds are strongly against your ever being able to achieve it—in fact, they are practically nil. One needs only to look at income distribution in the country to see that fewer than 5 percent of the people own more than half of the wealth and that fewer and fewer people manage to get their heads above water enough even to own their own homes. There is little room at the top, the competition is fierce and bloody, and making it to the top is only the beginning of the struggle. You may not stay there for any length of time; if you do, it will be only through merciless competition. The cruelest joke of all is that even if you did succeed, after years of consuming effort to become powerful and rich and managed to hold on to your wealth, it would probably not make you happy. Many people who have fulfilled the "power dream" found it empty and have given it up; the American Dream has become a dead-end street.

If your reaction is a suspicious "That's easy for you to say; you have power. I want mine and I am going after it!" I would certainly understand and wish you luck. In any case, I am not advocating powerlessness or meekness. On the contrary, I feel that people should be as powerful as they can possibly be. I am speaking specifically against a certain form of power I call Control, which depends on exploiting and manipulating others. Control makes power available to only a few because it is based on taking it away from the many. Control is a pathetic, parasitic leeching of other people's strength to our own temporary advantage. I am speaking *for* the other side of power, which we all have within our immediate reach: the substantial, tangible, usable, durable powers of love, intuition, communication, and cooperation which can get us what we want and make us genuinely happy.

PART ONE:
Control

1

THE AMERICAN POWER DREAM

A few years ago, when I started writing this book, there was an upsurge of interest in power. Books on power like *The Power Broker,* by Robert A. Caro; *Power and Innocence,* by Rollo May; *Tales of Power,* by Carlos Castaneda; *Power, the Inner Experience,* by David McClelland; *The Price for Power,* by Arnold Hutschnecker, *On Personal Power,* by Carl Rogers; *The Abuse of Power,* by Newfield and Du Brill; *Power, Inc.,* by Mintz and Cohen, and many others, appeared continuously over a span of a few years. Of all the books on power, Michael Korda's *Power! How to Get It, How to Use It* was most interesting to me because it was both readable and sophisticated. It became a major best-seller because it spoke directly and clearly about the every-day realities of power as it operates in the mainstream of American life: the business world. Almost simultaneously with Korda's book, *How to Win Through Intimidation,* by Robert Ringer, also became an instant best-seller. Ringer's book is less intricate and thoughtful, more down-to-earth; the redneck's version of Korda's book. They both faithfully portray the kind of power relations which are all too typical for people, whether they are in business or not; for competitive business practices permeate our life.

Korda's book is an encyclopedia of observations about power behavior. I'm sure that his book has been read by everybody who is anybody in business, and I imagine that it has had a definite effect on power behavior in industry and commerce. Korda points to the importance of the brief-cases, watches, shoes, and clothes that people wear. He proposes that ears, noses, eyes, and feet are as important as where we sit in our own or someone else's office, how we move around at an office party, or how we answer the phone. He claims that all of these items are related to our level of power.

As we read Korda's observations of the superficialities of power behavior, we soon become aware of his more profound convictions. Early in the book, he quotes Heinrich von Treitschke: "Your neighbor, even though he may look upon you as his natural ally against another power which is feared by you both, is always ready at the first opportunity, as soon as it can be done with safety, to better himself at your expense. . . . Whoever fails to increase his power must decrease his if others increase theirs."

It is interesting to note how Korda, as so many other writers on the subject, wants to appear to be simply a reporter on matters of power; one who, himself, is above prejudice or preference. However, his approach is thoroughly slanted. In a March 1977 *Mainliner* interview with Joseph Poindexter, Korda defines power extremely narrowly as "the ability to control people, events, and oneself. . . . In a word, power is control." He also subtly but very definitely favors power abuse: "[A] notion of power I'm fond of *is that it is the extent to which you can make others wait for you as opposed to having to wait for them.*" (emphasis mine)

In his definition of power as *strictly a matter of control over others,* Korda follows the most common view. This all-pervasive notion is shared by most writers on the subject; the only disagreement seems to be whether power (Control) is good or bad, desirable or undesirable, Korda seems to admire people who are powerful but use their power over others smoothly and elegantly. For instance, he speaks almost lovingly of David Mahoney, the fifty-two-year-old chairman, president, and chief executive of Norton Simon, Inc., whose office "seems to have been designed to reflect the presence of power and money, in a quiet, self-assured style that is peculiar to late-twentieth-century America." He describes stainless steel and leather furniture, enormous abstract paintings; everything is solid and expensive, ". . . What makes the difference is money." He describes his eyes: large, intelligent, hypnotic, unblinking, cold, shrewd. Mahoney seems to exemplify Korda's ideal of power and success. Impressive offices, limousines, obedient and efficient employees, expense accounts, servants; in short, maximum control, minimum bother.

Korda's almost fawning admiration of David Mahoney is in sharp contrast with his disdain for ineffectual uses of Control. He believes that all of the power abuses committed by the Nixon White House were really the result of those men's "inner sense of worthlessness that made them fear that they had no right to be there, and might at any moment be found out, [which] revealed [them] as weak and ordinary men." He faults Nixon and his people for being possessed by a high level of self-pity, and "self-pity is not an emotion one connects with a sense of power. What is more, it led inevitably to blunders, inefficiency, and bad management. A truly powerful group of men might well have succeeded in burglarizing the office of Daniel Ellsberg's psychiatrist, or tapping Larry O'Brien's telephone—neither feat would have seemed insufferably difficult." In other words, Korda seems to feel that the Nixon White House was simply not effective in its use of power. Had they been effective, it seems that Korda would be in awe of them, and would not give a second thought to the damage they might have inflicted upon the American people. Had they been successful, Korda's attitude might be similar to his attitude about David Mahoney.

Korda doesn't appreciate crude exhibitions of power, and in example after example in his book he endorses maneuvers for the same goal—Control—as long as they are subtle, elegant, smooth, and *effective*. He is a sophisticate of power abuse; it's good to have power and to use it to control others, as long as it is done with style. Most stylish, of course, is the capacity to appear to have no power at all while being all-powerful: "The contemporary American's type of power is to pretend that one has none."

In contrast to Korda's veiled support of power abuse, Robert Ringer's *Winning Through Intimidation* gets right down to brass tacks and tells us at the onset that there are only three types of people, all three of which are out to screw you. Type #1 lets you know from the beginning that he is out to get all of your chips and attempts to do just that. Type #2 assures you that he's not interested in getting your chips and implies that he wants to be fair with you. He then follows through and tries to grab all of your chips anyway. Type #3 assures you that he is not interested in getting any of your chips, and he sincerely means it. In the end, due to any number of reasons, he, like Type #1 and #2, still ends up trying to grab your chips. His motto is "I really didn't mean to cut off your hand at the wrist, but I had no choice when you reached for your chips." According to Ringer, there are no Type #4 people: your choice is between #1, #2, and #3.

Ringer calls these three types his professors at "Screw U." If asked, I imagine Korda would seem to be ambivalent about just which, of these three, he particularly prefers; Ringer's mind is made up. Type #1, the honest (because straightforward) vulture is his clear favorite, since he would rather deal with a straightforward competitor than with a Type #2, who has every intention of screwing him, but disguises his intentions successfully enough to confuse his victim. Type #2, the mystifying vulture, may be Michael Korda's favorite, since he seems to feel that the trick is "to make people do what you want them to, and *like* it, to persuade them that they want what *you* want."

Korda and Ringer reflect what is going on in a very large and influential portion of the world of business. In this world, in which power has become simply, as Korda says, a "means of protecting ourselves against the cruelty, indifferences and ruthlessness of other men," peopled by types #1, #2, and #3, it would be foolish to ignore the kinds of power and its uses which are described by Korda and Ringer. After all, as Korda says in the *Mainliner* interview, "There is a fixed amount applicable to a given situation at a given time, and what you have diminishes what someone else has by that amount. Your gain is someone else's loss; your failure, someone else's victory."

It is from this same perspective that R. H. Morrisson, president of Securities Management Associates, wrote *Why Sons of Bitches Succeed and Why Nice Guys Fail In Small Business,* in which Chapter Two will show you "how to screw your employees first, that is before they screw you, how to keep them smiling on low pay, how to maneuver them into low paid jobs, and how to hire and fire so that you always make money." Chapter Eight will teach you "how to squeeze your competitors dry, how to play the game the way the Rockefellers, IBM's, General Motors and other Big Boys play it—to win." With the S.O.B. techniques in this chapter, "you can bury the competition and laugh, all the way to the bank." In Chapter Four, you will "discover how to win every ass-kicking contest you get into with them by out-smarting and out-bullshitting them every step of the way." This book confirms Korda's and Ringer's view of the world. As Morrisson says, "Every small businessman needs this book, even the nice guys, to protect themselves against the S.O.B.'s." He's not particular about who he sells the book to: a buck is a buck, whether from an S.O.B. or a sucker.

Looking out for your neighbor is plain foolish. There is no worth to fairness, conscience, generosity, sharing, or co-operation. Only one thing really matters: Control and the accumulation of power, preferably in the form of money.

Indeed, we are so immersed in this world that it is hard to see what is wrong with this approach. Control, power, and money do seem awfully attractive don't they? What else can make us feel as good? Who can argue that it is better to be without them? What else are we to pursue? Love, fairness, and generosity *sound* good, but can we feed our children on them?

In his latest book, *Success!,* Korda provides us with a handy set of guidelines that should settle your questions once and for all. Here is a summary of what he says:

It's okay to be greedy and ambitious. It's okay to look out for Number One. It's okay to be Machiavellian (if you can get away with it). It's okay to recognize that honesty is not always the best policy (provided you don't go around saying so). It's okay to have a good time and to be a winner. And yes, it's always okay to be rich.

Unfortunately, most people who are trying to make their lives work all too often assume this is the best path to achievement. By committing themselves to this type of competitive life-style, they are leaving behind all of the different options in which achievement of power doesn't depend on reducing someone else's, or risking one's own, in a competitive gamble. At the same time, people who commit themselves to the American Power Dream will find that the heartless attitudes about people and their feelings required by this approach have many silent consequences: alienated marriages, nasty divorces, ruined friendships, sullen, angry, drug-taking children, ulcers, hypertension, heart disease. Finally they will discover that, after spending their "productive" years feverishly pursuing Control power and neglecting their intimate relationships, the next generation of competitors will be glad to give them the same treatment they so enthusiastically dished out to others. In fact, in his book, Korda himself provides us with a chilling and underhanded step-by-step method for young company men to get rid of aging executives, in a section titled "Men must endure their going hence."

Thinking that you can become powerful in Korda's, Ringer's and Morrisson's games is like walking into a crooked gambling casino hoping that you can make a killing. Everything is stacked against you; you are like an unsuspecting lamb being lured into the shearing shed by the smiling faces of those who are preparing to fleece you. Your chances of winning are very, very low. If, by some chance you *do* win, you have to spend the rest of your life hovering over your spoils like a vulture waiting for the next kill. Do you really want to live that way?

The ultimate irony is that, of late, Robert Ringer, who developed the Ringer method for automobile sales and who tells us how to intimidate and screw our neighbor has gone from Type #1 professor at Screw U to becoming a philosopher for "free enterprise."

In his latest book, *Restoring the American Dream,* he upgrades his act and resells it to us in a new package, in the form of a treatise on freedom, individualism, and the American Dream. According to him, the American Dream is indeed dead or close to dead. He blames this death on politicians, government, and the overregulation of our business people.

According to Ringer, "America can't afford not to have rich people, for they are the very backbone of productivity, employment, and a better life for all." He wants us to hand what is left of our dream to the rich folk, who have already succeeded in beating it to within an inch of its life so that they can suck it completely dry once and for all.

The aplomb with which Ringer states his views can only be understood if one remembers that he is, first and foremost, a salesman. It all sounds so plausible somehow. How did the rich become the backbone of productivity? What happened to the workers?

Let us not forget that if the American Dream is dead it was killed by the greedy, the selfish individualists, the robber barons, the multinational corporations who in the name of free enterprise stop at nothing as they pursue power, control, and the almighty dollar. Government regulation is only a feeble, ineffectual effort to stop them.

Years ago, when I had achieved success and began to look the American Dream in the face, I had been feeling mighty proud of all my accomplishments. I did not see how much of what I was accomplishing was the result of my optimal position to make use of resources which were mostly not my own. I was the privileged white male child of educated parents in a land and time of plenty. It seemed to me—and others in similarly privileged positions—that with a little hard work anybody could make a go of it. Those that didn't were either lazy or dumb. I didn't realize that many other people worked twice as hard as I did and didn't succeed at all. I didn't know that people just as smart, just as hardworking as myself went through life unable to keep up with their basic needs and spent their "golden" years in abject poverty—if they even lived that long. I happened to be on the top levels of a global pyramid which funneled its resources in my direction, and I was not aware of it.

In other words, I was a self-satisfied fool. I was cheating without knowing it; my power was not really mine. It had a large portion of its source elsewhere, that I had mistakenly assumed came solely from me. Inevitably, I was headed in the direction of disappointment. I wasn't really entitled to the feelings of mastery and power that I enjoyed. They were based on the unwitting usurpation of other people's birthright. As I became more aware of the realities of my position on the "ladder of success," I had more and more difficulty when trying to smugly assert my unfair privilege because I saw that my power was based on the powerlessness of others.

I began to glimpse the realities of my privileged dream as a result of the civil-rights movement. I had known, of course, that blacks were suppressed in this country, but I had not stopped to think about how their oppression benefited me, personally. As blacks rioted, became uppity, pressed their advantage, and began to get better jobs and salaries, I was able to feel the squeeze of their demands. My cleaning woman wanted more pay and wasn't being friendly about it. The docile Negroes who used to do menial jobs for me became angry blacks in jobs which, I thought, they weren't able to "handle" effectively. Still, my well-insulated suburban life was barely touched by these developments; they provided me with a preliminary taste of what was to come, and I could accept them with a liberal attitude.

The full reality of my wholly unearned personal privilege was served up to me by the women's movement. Women all around me began to stop cooking, doing dishes, taking care of children. They started taking up space in conversations and questioning my right to dominate every situation with my presence and opinions. It was clear now that the liberal attitudes that got me by the Black Power movement were not going to work with women. If I was going to be serious about women's rights I would actually have to *give up* something.

To my surprise, I found that hard to take. My friends say that I had to be forced to let go of my grip on things, finger by clawlike finger. I was lucky to have loving—as well as determined—teachers in this matter. Each concession of power on my part was rewarded and followed by a new, demanding lesson.

I discovered that giving up privilege, though uncomfortable and frightening, can be exhilarating as well. I began to notice that being fair often feels better than getting my way and that the pleasure of sharing what there is makes up for having to do with less. Eventually, I also saw how giving up privilege caused people to treat me more lovingly and respectfully.

From then on it was a chillingly simple matter to realize that my privilege extended beyond blacks and women. I had an unfair advantage over young and old people, gay people, disabled people, fat people, single people, but above all over the vast numbers of poor people in this country and the world over. The illusion that I was entitled to that advantage dissolved, and this new awareness radically changed my view of myself and the world.

Let's face it: we affluent Middle Americans have been on a free ride for a long time; a free ride provided to us by many hardworking people for one thing, and by the good earth for another. Until recently, we took at will, without any opposition, with only a few farseeing prophets making a silly fuss about it. But recently the various liberation and environmental movements have put a crimp in our style. And coming soon—actually here, right around the corner— the greatest blow: we will run out of easily appropriated natural resources. Cheap oil is gone, and therefore cheap energy is gone forever. The inexpensive, docile work force we have depended upon is fast receding. Our renewable resources are not renewing themselves, and our nonrenewable resources are dwindling. Conservationists are fighting further environmental destruction-for-profit. Women want their due; our racial minorities want what's coming to them. Workers want a fair wage, and we are now forced to look elsewhere in the world for easily exploitable labor. The horn of plenty is emptying. The free ride is over. As we enter the coming age of scarcity, our feelings of power can no longer be based on those ample sources we are so accustomed to tapping. We'll have to look elsewhere for the energy to sustain us.

We will have to grow up and develop powers of our own; powers which emanate from each of us, rather than from external sources. We will have to let go of mother's nipple and share what there is with our clamoring brothers and sisters, all of whom deserve her milk as richly as we do. Those of us who refuse will find themselves embattled against overwhelming pressures and will have to use drastic measures to defend the indefensible. In the end, only a few will be able to hold on to their unfair advantage; a few always do. The question for everyone is: "Which side of this struggle do you want to be on?" This book's task is to document the validity of the obvious answer.

We will have to give up the illusion of power and plentiful energy which we have been living on. We will have to walk, bicycle, work, sweat, take shorter showers, wear sweaters, wait in line, recycle, conserve, carpool, ride public transportation, share, discuss, be outvoted, organize, demand our rights, and respect the rights of others. We'll have to work harder and we'll have to learn to do with less. Nevertheless, we need not be frightened because, as a friend puts it, "Power is in everything, omnipresent, locked in every cell, every molecule and atom. It naturally radiates from all matter. We are powerless because we curtail, control and disbelieve in ourselves and each other". There is a source of power and pleasure hidden from our view for every one we are in the process of losing.

As I grow away from my delusions of power, I realize that I still want to be powerful, but now my goal is being strong without abuse. I want to cooperate with other people so we can all grow powerful together. I don't want to treat any person, living thing, or portion of the earth as my exclusive property, to be used at will for my selfish purposes.

I want to put in as much as I take out of all situations. I want to speak with the eloquence of a poet and think with the wisdom of a sage. I want to live comfortably with my close loving friends and family. I want to travel, be warm in the winter and cool in the summer, enjoy hard work, eat delicious and healthy food, and rejoice in my leisure. I want to be loved by many, hated by none. I want to be fair, considerate, and neighborly. I want to be guided by my conscience in all my actions. I want to grow old and crusty and be respected for my life and deeds. I want to be appreciated by my co-workers and business competitors. I want to be fully alive to my powers and to the portion of the earth I inhabit. I want all of those things without power-playing others, without abusing power, and I want you to have the same. And not just you, but all of us who inhabit this planet, from now on, forever.

The alternative offered in this book—*The Other Side of Power*—is based on the belief that it is possible to be powerful, happy, and alive, to have close loving friends, to be appreciated by one's co-workers, business competitors, or employees—and at the same time to be fair, considerate, and be guided by one's conscience in all of one's actions.

First we will have to understand what Control Power is, how it works, and how to prevent its use by ourselves and others. Then we will look into giving up Control and what replaces Control when we give it up. We will see how all of this looks in practical everyday situations so that, if we choose, we can explore the other side of power for ourselves.

In the next chapter I will speak of Mark and Joan and their struggles. At first it may appear that their problems are sexual, but my point will be that the real reason for their difficulties is power and control. Let us see what Control Power looks like in people's everyday lives.

2

CONTROL IN
OUR EVERYDAY LIVES

Mark

Driving home from work on the traffic-choked freeway, Mark's thoughts wove around the cheerful voice coming from the radio. "Have patience," the announcer mockingly reassured him, after the traffic report, "you'll soon be in the arms of your loving mate . . . if not, perhaps a stiff drink will do." Mark became aware that he was thinking of sex . . . again.

Sex with Joan had not been good lately. Increasingly, over the last year, she wasn't interested. On the contrary, she turned away from him when he joined her in bed, she didn't feel well, or she fell asleep early. Every so often they did make love, but it wasn't the same.

As he thought about it, feelings of anger were mixed with desire and a sense of humiliation. Damn, he was horny, and he didn't like to be begging. He felt very angry.

The more Joan avoided his sexual advances, the more his interest became almost obsessive. Joan seemed determined not to warm up to him unless things were exactly right for her. All the dishes done, plenty of time to relax, nothing to spoil her mood. On a working day, things just did not come together that way anymore. Why was she being so difficult? When they met, two years ago, sex was spontaneous: before dinner, after dinner, even sometimes during dinner, watching television, in the middle of the night, before running off to work. Joan was certainly being difficult nowadays. Maybe tonight . . .

As he walked into the house, he made a mental note to be careful. She stood by the stove, stirring something in a saucepan. He reminded himself to stay away from her magnetically attractive sexy spots. "Hi, honey," he said as he kissed her lightly on the cheek.

He knew she liked to talk about things. And so did he. What was going on with the children? How are things developing at her new part-time job? He resisted an impulse to turn on the television and watch the evening news. As they spoke, he became sexually aroused. Forgetting himself, Mark walked over to Joan, holding her from behind and tenderly cupping his hands over her breasts. Almost immediately, he realized he had made a mistake. He felt her stiffen. "Damn! Why does she have to be so touchy?" He decided to withdraw. He would wait until after dinner. He reminded himself to make no sexual moves at all until then.

After dinner, Mark turns on the news, Joan wants to object but doesn't want to nag. Mark does the dishes while Joan talks on the phone with a friend. When everything finally calms down, while they are watching the tube, he looks at her, asks: "Do you want to smoke some marijuana?" She looks back at him, thinks for a second:

"No, thanks. Go ahead if you want."

A flash of anger. "Damn! Damn! Damn!", "That is it!" he thinks. "I'm not going to try again. If there's gonna be sex tonight, it'll have to be her move, not mine." With one eye on the TV he reaches for the newspaper and sulkily rolls and lights a joint. A half hour later, without saying anything, he gets up.

"Going to bed so soon?" she asks sweetly.

"Yes, I'm tired, see you later . . . maybe," he says bitterly.

Soon she joins him in bed. She seems to have softened. Hope rises in his chest. Maybe . . . He turns around, thrusting his leg between her thighs.

Oops! Definitely the wrong move. Her legs clamp

around his knee and she turns belly-down on the bed. He sits bolt upright.

"What the hell is the matter with you?"

"What do you mean?"

"You know damn well what I mean. Are you turning frigid on me?"

"I just don't want to have sex like this."

"Why not?"

"Sex is all you want from me. I need more, and you just haven't got any of what I want."

"Jesus Christ, I'm busting my gut to do the right thing. What do you want anyway?"

"I want you to love me, not just to fuck me."

"Oh for God's sake, I give up. I don't know what I have to do to convince you that I love you. I want you, and I think about you all the time. What else do you want?"

He turns from her. "Good night, sleep well." Fleeting thoughts of forcing himself on her cross his mind, but he dismisses them.

Joan says nothing and turns off the light. They both fall asleep as a black cloud hovers over their bed.

Joan

As Joan cut up some vegetables for dinner, she realized that Mark would be soon coming home. She was tired and somewhat grumpy; things had not gone well at her new job. She was looking forward to Mark's arrival; but with the pleasant expectation, she sensed an accompanying feeling of anxiety. She didn't pay attention to it, but it was a subtle, unpleasant sensation which had been coming over her almost every time she thought about Mark. Still, mostly she eagerly looked forward to his cheerful smile and his mellow, booming voice. She heard the car drive up into their parking space, heard the car door slam; a few seconds later, Mark was at the door.

She greeted him and felt glad to see him. She hoped he

would come up and kiss her, but as he approached, she felt that peculiar crawly feeling again, just slightly spoiling her gladness. She felt his light touch and subtle kiss and saw with pleasure that he was going to sit and talk with her. She loved having him look at her while she was busy doing something. She was glad that she had decided to cook one of his favorite dishes. This would be a good dinner. They would talk and laugh and have a good time.

As she stirred the mushrooms into the stew, he got up and walked toward her. She had been hoping that he would come closer and touch her. Suddenly she froze; his anticipated embrace had become a rude grab for her breasts. That subtle anxiety which had plagued her became full panic. "Oh, my God, here we go again," she thought. Her mind and body went blank as she concentrated on the sauce.

The next thing she knew, Mark was gone. She could hear him tinkering around in the workroom. She was definitely scared and worried. Something terrible was happening to her feelings for Mark. It wasn't that she didn't love him; she just didn't seem to want sex with him, and he grew more insistent every day. She didn't like his approach; it was crude, rude, and lacked any romance. It was a real turn-off and made her sick. He was no longer willing to just sit, talk, watch TV, in a tight, loving embrace. All he wanted was sex, sex, sex. Whenever she tried to get him to just be with her, he either ran out of the room, turned on the TV, or made a pass. She realized that the blame could not be placed entirely on him. Maybe things could be smoothed out. She was going to try hard to respond to his wish to have sex.

During dinner and after, Mark seemed remote. Joan tried to make friendly conversation and he responded, but there was no warmth in his voice. Was he angry, or had he just lost interest in being sexy? Maybe she was making a big deal out of this. Maybe he was OK. She decided not to worry, and relax.

Sitting next to him on the couch, she felt a faint stirring of sexual interest. She really did enjoy Mark, and remembered how passionately they had made love in the past. In the middle of one of her reveries, Mark looked up significantly, "Do you want to smoke some marijuana?" His look took her by surprise. He was up to something, and she didn't like it. She thought for a second and resented the implicit expectation in his question. "Turn on, loosen up, let's fuck." Without thinking further, she declined his offer. She noticed his hurt look, became unsure of her decision. If he passed her the joint, she'd accept.

But Mark seemed to completely withdraw now. He lit up, smoked his dope without offering her any, and got up abruptly. She feigned surprise.

"Going to bed so soon?"

"Yes," he said. "I'm tired. See you later . . . maybe."

As he went off to the bedroom, she heard that word "maybe" resonate in her ears. Was that a sarcastic comment, or was it a hopeful invitation? She was getting very jumpy about him, wasn't she? She decided, once again, not to make a big thing out of what seemed to her to be an unnecessarily snide comment.

Having watched the end of the program, Joan turned off the TV and the lights and tiptoed to the bedroom. Maybe Mark was still awake. Maybe they would talk sweetly for a while. She looked at Mark in bed. He seemed to be asleep. Good, she thought. We can cuddle all night, and I will feel loving and physically close to him. Then we can have sex tomorrow morning before he goes to work, like we used to.

She took off her clothes, decided not to wear a nightgown, and pulled back the covers. As she slid next to him, he turned around unexpectedly. Joan was startled because she had thought he was asleep, and her knees instinctively clamped together as he thrust his leg between hers.

Before she recovers from her confusion, he sits up. His face twists with rage and his fists clench as he yells something at her which she answers without thinking. She feels panicky. Then she grows cold and calculating as she answers his accusations automatically, defensively; all resolve to be loving gone, replaced by anger and hurt.

When Mark's fury finally runs out and he sinks back under the covers, she is glad to go to sleep. She feels sorry for the both of them. "Maybe I should go see a sex therapist," she thinks.

Sleep comes to her easily. Throughout the night they drift slowly toward each other, touching here and there, first lightly, and then, eventually, holding each other as closely as they ever had. In their dreams they make love to each other.

Power Plays

This example specifically illustrates a typical conflict between two people.

It's not that Joan and Mark don't love each other anymore. They do, and they are still sexually attracted to each other. But something has gone wrong. What once flowed easily and joyously between them has been interrupted. Both of them are puzzled, hurt, angry. Both feel the other is mostly to blame. Before the trouble began, they were in love. Joan had never been so sexually turned on; Mark had never been so tender and thoughtful. At first the problem went unnoticed amidst the busy days and tired nights. But little by little, over the last year, a pattern emerged of which neither was clearly aware. The free and loving exchange between them began to include occasional controlling transactions. One evening as they lay in bed, Mark ignored Joan's lack of interest and forcibly made love to her. She didn't really resist, although she made sure not to respond in a big way. The next time they were in bed together, she rolled away from him in a tight impenetrable ball. Later in the week, Joan had planned a quiet Sunday morning in bed. She visualized how they would lie around and just talk; how he would get up and make coffee and prepare some English muffins and jam. But before she could even wake up he was out of bed, working in the garden, and soon she got up, too. Nights later, while Joan was asleep, Mark caressed and kissed her and she became aroused. Before she knew it, they were having intercourse. She half-enjoyed it and half-resented it, but the next time he fondled her in the middle of the night, she woke up, turned over on her stomach, and went back to sleep.

Over the months, Mark's attempts to manipulate Joan into sex escalated, and her maneuvers to resist escalated right along. Joan's attempts at creating intimate nonsexual times were equally unsuccessful.

On the evening described earlier, Mark attempts a number of controlling maneuvers. First he hides his desires for sex as he comes into the house. He assumes that if she knew what he wanted, she would turn him down. So he controls what he does and says in order to control her. Even though he would rather watch television, he engages in a conversation with her, which is an attempt to give her what she wants—not particularly out of affection, but with the anticipation that this will get him what he wants. Again he is trying to control her. Later, he forgets his resolve and acts out of impulse; but when he discovers that the impulse turns Joan off, he tries another tactic. He withdraws completely, hoping thereby to create an interest on her part, spurred by his absence. He carries this tactic through dinner.

Next, he hits on a new idea. "Maybe if she got stoned, she'd loosen up." She catches on and refuses his offer. Now he sulks; that'll make her feel guilty. When she comes to bed, he pretends to be asleep; this will prove to her that he doesn't give a damn. Maybe that'll work. When she seems to be responding with some warmth, he forgets himself and again grabs at her. Seeing that he has failed once more, he now tries a cruder approach. He insults her and accuses her of being frigid. He tries to arouse her guilt. He attempts to frighten her into submission. Eventually, he withdraws into another sulk as he fantasizes the ultimate sexual power play.

As we see the feelings and experiences that Joan goes through, matters look different. She has developed a low-key, almost instinctive fear of his sexual advances. A series of similar evenings have created an expectation of trouble. She becomes anxious anytime he makes an approach. As a consequence, his moves—whether they are controlling and manipulating, or direct and honest—meet with the identical reaction: a tightening, a withdrawal, a blocking of his every move, passive resistance. She is now intent on remaining in control, on not being manipulated; she knows of no other way of getting what she wants, and neither does he. They are locked in a struggle for power and know of no way out of their embattled positions. He finds himself trying to manipulate in order to get what he wants, and she finds herself almost automatically refusing it. Both of them get nothing.

In the past, Mark's maneuvers have succeeded. He has managed to distract Joan, or to create a need for him, or to cause her to submit out of guilt or fear. But these tactics aren't working anymore. They seldom do, after a while. People don't like to be controlled, and manipulation eventually arouses a strong will to resist. Struggle ensues, energy is wasted, powerlessness results. Mark's and Joan's situation is just one example of people power-playing each other.

Let us look at Mark's side of the power struggle: Mark wants sex, Joan doesn't; that's what he sees. He may go about getting it in a direct and crude manner by just simply grabbing for it, or he may also, either separately or at the same time, be much more subtle about it. We saw him trying to sell Joan on sex by setting the scene for hours. We saw him hide his feelings, try to arouse guilt, fake interest, withdraw, try to get her high, and we saw him sulk. When Mark's subtle approach doesn't work, he is liable to try a cruder one (as in the case of his rape fantasy, before they fell asleep, or when he clenched his fists as he yelled at her.)

If you have a loaf of bread which I want, I can simply grab it from you and eat it while I pin you to the ground. That's the crude approach. I also can get that loaf of bread through other means. I can convince you that it is mine, that I have more right to it than you. I can impress you with how hungry I am, so that you'll give it up out of guilt or shame. I can scare you out of it by speaking ominously of what might happen if you don't share it with me. I can smilingly kid you out of it.

In our everyday lives, we are controlled primarily through subtle means. We are seldom clearly aware of how these methods accomplish their purpose even if we use them on others ourselves. Force is not the immediate basis for their success. Instead, they rely on our obedience, our unwillingness to challenge authority out of fear, politeness, or our incapacity to know and ask for what we want.

All of the maneuvers used by Mark and Joan, subtle or crude, offensive or defensive, fall under the definition of power plays and are a major focus of this book. Power plays are the tools of Control and competition. When they are introduced into a loving, cooperative relationship they affect it profoundly.

Let us look into another situation where power plays are used habitually.

Meanwhile, Back at the Office

It's 4:00, one hour before quitting time. You've worked hard all day; you've had two fifteen-minute coffee breaks and a thirty-minute lunch. As you expectantly look forward to the end of the workday, your boss comes into the office, lays a folder on your desk, looks at you with a smile, and says, "These have to be done before tomorrow morning. OK?"

You hesitate, but answer automatically. "OK."

"Thanks," she says as she briskly turns around and leaves.

You pick up the folder and look at what's in it. It looks like an hour and a half's worth of work. You know you won't be able to finish it by 5:00. That means you'll have to stay longer, miss the early traffic, and be stuck in the heavy rush hour. You're low on gas and risk running out. You'll have to stop in the heavy traffic and buy some. You're confused, and angry. Yet, she asked if it was OK and you agreed: "OK?" she said, and you answered, "OK." How can you now turn around and make a fuss? Your mind is flooded with emotions and you can't think. All you know is that an hour and a half of work is to be done before tomorrow morning. You say to yourself, "Well, the faster you get into it, the faster you'll get finished. There's no point in wasting any time. You'll just have to stay longer if you do."

You have been power-played. Your boss has managed to get you to do something that you didn't want to do, something that she has no right to expect of you. And she has done it without laying a hand on you and with a smile, to boot. She relied on your obedience, unwillingness to challenge her, and subservience, to get you to do something which she knew perfectly well was unreasonable. Had you been more quick-witted, you would have said, "Wait, I'm not sure it's OK. Let me look at it." And, after having looked at it, you might have said, "Why do you bring me this so late? Why does it have to be done by tomorrow morning? Can't you get someone else to help?" And perhaps, "I don't have to work after five o'clock. I don't care if this has to be done before tomorrow morning. If it's so important, you should have given it to me earlier. Why don't you hire some temporary help? I need to be paid time and a half for this." Or even, "Why don't you do it yourself?"

Clearly, that type of behavior would be seen as insubordinate, rebellious, uncooperative; and if your job was one which could be easily filled by someone else, your boss might start thinking of firing you and replacing you with someone who's more "cooperative." The choice is not simple. What are you to do?

The confusion we feel in such situations is sensible. We want to be cooperative, good workers, reasonable. But we are often asked to be these things by people who have only themselves in mind and who would not hesitate to control us to their advantage. The only way to decide wisely and responsibly is to understand the situation better, by learning about power; how it is abused through crude and subtle power plays, and how it is used cooperatively and humanely. Only then can we know if what we are doing is out of obedience and submission or out of the free choice and the wish to be cooperative.

People have the right to work in an atmosphere where power plays like forced overtime aren't used, and where workers and employees alike ask for what they want, reasonably and fairly. Workers need the assurance that their willingness to work hard will not be abused or taken for granted, and bosses need to know that workers will be ready to work when needed and do it in the most productive way possible. Working situations like that are possible. In such a work setting, the boss would approach you very differently. She might come into your office and wait politely until you finish what you're doing. At this point, she might sit down and say, "I'm sorry to interrupt, but I would like to ask whether you can do some extra work today before you leave. It'll take about an hour and a half."

If you showed unhappiness with the request, she might say, "This is really important—can we make a deal? Perhaps you want to take some time off tomorrow morning." Or, "Would you do it just once, as a favor? I'll return the favor some other time." This cooperative request, free of power plays, might succeed in causing you to decide to do the work with a smile. If it did not, then you and your boss would discuss a creative solution to the problem—such as getting someone else, postponing the work, or taking it home. In the end, you and she would have a better working relationship based on mutual respect. It would be potentially more creative and productive, more likely to endure, and more satisfying to both.

These two approaches—the Control, power-play competitive mode—and the Other Side of Power—the loving, give-and-take, cooperative mode—describe the major issue in this book.

Let us begin by examining why we accept other people's control over us.

3

OBEDIENCE: WHY WE ACCEPT CONTROL BY OTHERS

Subtle power plays depend on our obedience, which is often mistaken for cooperation. Cooperation very often means going along, not arguing, and doing as others, who know better, tell us. President Nixon was very irritated with the press and the American public, who did not "cooperate" with his plans. The Vietnamese didn't cooperate with "Vietnamization," much to the annoyance of the U.S. military. The American colonists refused to pay their taxes and to "cooperate" with England. Today people aren't cooperating with the nuclear energy program. Later I will explain in detail how cooperation and obedience differ from each other. For now, let me give an example that illustrates how we are often talked into cooperation which is actually merely obedience.

You are sitting on a park bench, on a cool but sunny spring day, enjoying the early-morning sun. Your eyes are closed, and you feel the warm sunlight all over. You are happy and content as your mind drifts in a pleasant daydream. Suddenly a shadow is cast over you. You feel a chill, open your eyes, and see somebody standing there between you and the sun. He is dressed in suit and tie, good-looking, relaxed, graying at the temples. You smile and say, "Hi."

"Hi," he replies, but he doesn't move.

His face is against the sun, so you can't quite see his features. "He probably doesn't realize that he is obscuring the sun's warmth," you think to yourself.

"Excuse me, but you're standing in my light."

He answers, "I know."

You are puzzled. You take a closer look. He looks kindly but serious and does not seem to be challenging you. You move over, back into the sunlight. Now you can see his face; he is eyeing you with detached interest. He shifts his position and blocks your light again. Your confusion grows. You ask yourself, "Why is he doing this?" You assume that he has a good reason and that you are probably missing the point of his behavior. You don't want to offend this nice-looking man. You don't want any hassles. He looks friendly enough, but you are a little scared. There must be some mistake. You are probably overreacting. After all, he is only standing in your light. You close your eyes again, but you are getting annoyed.

After a few seconds, trying to sound calm, you ask, "Why are you standing in my light?"

He answers earnestly, "I'm glad you asked that question. It's very important that I do this. As a matter of fact, you must excuse me, but I have to do one other thing." He moves toward you and steps on your toe with his heel. You are shocked; undoubtedly he has made a mistake. He surely can't intentionally be stepping on your toe.

Suppressing a groan of pain, you say, "You're standing on my toe!"

He answers, "Yes, I know."

"Why?" you plead again, trying not to be visibly upset.

Very earnestly, he says, "This may be difficult for you to believe, but the reason that I'm standing on your toe is too complicated for you to understand. I cannot tell you why. All I can tell you is that it's essential to the economic health of our country. If we can't do this, the country will be plunged into a great energy crisis. And I would really appreciate it if you went along without any protest. Everyone else is and we can't have you interfere with our efforts to protect our economic security."

The man looks very serious. He is both earnest and

ominous. You think of yourself as a patriotic citizen. You are certainly aware of inflation and the energy crisis. You are not very experienced; you haven't really been able to understand the ins and outs of economics. In fact, you feel downright stupid about these matters. You repress a desire to ask him some questions for fear of exposing your ignorance. This man looks educated. He is obviously a winner, judging from his manner and dress—probably a successful businessman or college professor. "If you hadn't quit college, you might not be in this situation," you think. "You always have been lazy. Look at yourself—loafing on a park bench. . . . It doesn't hurt all that much to go along with him and do your part. If you made a tiny effort, you could easily tolerate the situation."

The man seems pleased, "You are a fine person: A credit to your parents. This nation owes you a great debt. Your children will be proud of you."

You are getting used to the pain. You look around and you see many people who are in the same situation you are. Wherever you look, kind-looking gentlemen in suits are stepping on people's toes. Everyone's smiling, or trying to smile. It really isn't so bad. You are beginning to feel better, knowing that you are doing the right thing, not creating a fuss; being appreciated by this man and knowing that you are helping with your civic-minded willingness to cooperate.

Off in the distance, you see a few people who seem to be protesting against toe-stepping. They've pushed the kindly gentlemen off their feet and they are running down the street, yelling, "Off our toes!"

You feel indignant. Why, there are even young boys and girls amongst the protesters. How can they corrupt children like this? Why are they uncooperative? How dare they endanger the energy future and the economy of our country? You are quite relieved when you see a line of policemen move in, stop the demonstration, and arrest those who don't peacefully disperse. Justice has been done.

You settle back in your seat, trying, once again, to enjoy

the sunlight. You close your eyes and concentrate on the warmth of the sun and the songs of the birds. You can hardly feel the pain under the stranger's foot. You drift into sleep and you dream of running through a meadow with wings on your feet. You feel free—you can fly. Suddenly you wake up. Startled, you realize that it was all a dream. You are back on the park bench, no one is standing on your foot; your new shoes are just too tight.

This allegory attempts to clarify the way in which we tend to accept and justify the subtle power plays which are perpetrated on us. We do not challenge the unpleasant things done to us by people who have power. We do not ask for proof of the need for the things that we tolerate. When we see others conform and go along, we assume that our objections are not justified. We forget our feelings and our fears. We believe people's lies. We don't approve of people who protest. In short, we become obedient. When in doubt, we doubt ourselves. If we don't understand something, we assume we are stupid. If we don't want to do something, we assume we are lazy. If we are too tired to challenge people who step on us, we assume we are weak. It takes more energy, skill, and courage than most of us have to challenge, ask questions, doubt authoritative statements, refuse to go along, openly criticize what everyone else is doing and defend our rights. We don't want to risk what we have by angering powerful people. To be obnoxious, disruptive, and stubborn is difficult and frightening. Instead, we go along quietly and we "cooperate," which, in this case, really means that we obey. We live in a dream within a dream, as R. D. Laing points out, where we have been hypnotized into accepting our oppression and then hypnotized again into forgetting that we were hypnotized in the first place.

The first step in becoming powerful without using power plays to control others is to learn to be disobedient. You are a free human being, and that freedom is powerful, if you will make use of it. Yet you spend much of your life being manipulated and pushed around by others. Refusing to be controlled against your will and judgment frees your own powers for whatever you may decide is good for you.

Obedience is a quality which many of us are taught; by our parents, by the schools, and by all the institutions of our childhood. We learn to do what others tell us to do without questioning it because we are, after all, only children. Obedience involves believing lies, not asking obvious questions, not saying what we want, not showing anger or sadness or some other feeling when we feel it, not demanding or defending our rights, smiling when we are unhappy, and, generally, just going along and not making waves.

After many years of obedience training, we become adults and we're expected to suddenly become individuals who think for ourselves, make our own decisions, are not easily manipulated, and do not take other people's words to represent the truth unless so demonstrated. As "red-blooded Americans," we are supposed to grow up to trust our own opinions and pursue our own welfare in our own way with a clear eye and firm resolve. Unfortunately, for many of us, that is very difficult, given our childhood training. We were told that obedience is a good quality, and we grow up to be obedient to authority, to people who speak as if they knew what they were doing, to people who tell us what's right and what's wrong, what we want and what we don't want, what's good for us and what isn't good for us, and to devious manipulations and lies. If we are women, we learn to obey men. If we're citizens, we learn to obey "authorities": leaders, scientists, the police, and our politicians. If we're workers, we learn to obey our bosses. If we are soldiers, we learn to obey our officers, regardless of what incredible and horrible things we may be asked to do.

Stanley Milgram wrote *Obedience to Authority,* the now-famous study which exposes the serious problem of obedience. In this experiment, ordinary people like you and me were hired to participate in a "learning" experiment. In the experiment, the learner was to memorize some words. You, the teacher, were to shock the learner if the learner made a mistake. Every time the learner made a mistake, you were instructed to push the next highest switch to increase the shock by 15 volts. The lowest shock was 15 volts, and the highest 450 volts. As the shock switches increased in voltage, they were labeled: "Intense shock (255 volts)," "Extreme intensity shock (311 volts)," "Danger: severe shock (375 volts)," and "XXX (450 volts)."

The learner was actually an actor (unbeknownst to the teacher) and at the higher levels of "shock" was instructed to scream and protest loudly.

For instance:

> At 300 volts: Agonized scream. "I absolutely refuse to answer any more. Get me out of here." "You can't hold me here, get me out. Get me out of here!"
>
> 330 volts: Intense and prolonged, agonized scream. "Let me out of here. Let me out of here. My heart is bothering me. Let me out, I tell you." (Hysterically). "Let me out of here, let me out of here! You have no right to hold me here. Let me out! Let me out! Let me out of here! Let me out! Let me out!"

The only person who was not an actor in this experiment was the teacher, the real subject in the experiment. As the learner made mistake after mistake and the "teacher" hesitated to increase the shock, the experimenter (also again, an actor), dressed in a lab coat, would say, "Please continue . . ." If the "teacher" was still hesitant, he would add, "The experiment requires that you continue. . . . It is absolutely essential that you continue. . . . You have no other choice—you *must* go on."

Now you probably would guess that you and most people would refuse to shock another person under these conditions. Well, guess again. About one of three of the very average people who participated in the experiment "shocked" the learner all the way to 450 volts—even after the learner seemed unconscious! And when they weren't actually administering the "shocks," but just administering the word test while another person did the electrocuting, nine out of ten went along all the way to the top of the scale.

"Not me!" you are probably saying to yourself. "I am sure I wouldn't be one of those." I am not nearly so sure of myself. Obedience to authority is deeply ingrained in our behavior; it is a basic program which few of us escape though we'd like to think that we do. Under the right circumstances, I know that I would be hard put not to do things I find repugnant, rather than to be disobedient—especially if they were introduced gradually, and I seemed to have no choice. Just how effective that combination of gradual, subtle introduction of abuse combined with lack of choice, backed by violence can be, was amply demonstrated in Nazi Germany, where a whole country of civilized people went along—cheerfully, it seems—with the Holocaust. What would you have done in Berlin in 1939? Would you have rebelled or would *you* have obeyed? What are you doing today? Are you going along, or are you disobeying?

Actually, obedience is a quality which we are told is admirable in children. Many of us would be embarrassed and insulted if someone said that a child of ours is disobedient. I believe otherwise, and pride myself that I have raised two disobedient children.

They are disobedient in that they are very unlikely to go along with authority figures and do as they are told without asking why. As you read this, you might think: "Well, he must have raised a couple of brats. Psychologists' children are usually that way anyway." However, my children are not bratty, sassy, sneaky, or obnoxious. They are honest, polite, and hardly ever do anything that really displeases people around them. They simply are children who want to know why they are doing what is being asked of them. They aren't likely to buckle under power plays, crude or subtle.

They love me and want to please me, but that doesn't mean that they are willing to go along with something that I or anyone else asks them to do "just because."

We are so used to thinking of obedience as a virtue that the notion of encouraging disobedience might seem extremely wrong and dangerous. But civil disobedience is a time-honored tradition, and has been a part of every worthwhile movement in our history.

Oppression is often supported by laws and traditions. Wanting to change those situations requires the will to disobey. The ousting of McCarthy and Nixon, the civil-rights movement, the establishment of trade unions, and, of course, our own revolution, were all based on civil disobedience. The defeat of nuclear power will require civil disobedience as well.

"But, what if disobedience were a trait of the whole population? Wouldn't that bring chaos and violence? What about law and order?"

Disobedience is not necessarily a rebellious, violent trait, though it *can* be that—and at times needs to be that. I am speaking mostly of gentle disobedience that comes from self-respect and an ironclad commitment to be lovingly critical of oneself and others, to not go along with what we don't agree with and to ask, "Why?" over and over again until we are satisfied.

Obedience and the Enemy

Why are some people strongly inclined to obey authority and some aren't? Is it a matter of willpower, or are some people born weak and others strong? What causes that important difference in people's character which determines whether they will accept domination or challenge it?

To answer this question, it is useful to have a rudimentary knowledge of Transactional Analysis. As you probably know, Eric Berne, the founder of Transactional Analysis, saw people as being divided into three ego states: the Parent, the Adult, and the Child. These ego states are three ways in which a person can behave. A more complete but brief description of this theory can be found in my book, *Scripts People Live.* For a more complete description of the theory of Transactional Analysis, see *Beyond Games and Scripts* by Eric Berne. Basically, a person can act in one of these three ways:

The Parent—the person who tells people what's right or wrong and what to do. The Parent can be nurturing, taking care of people, and trying to protect them against harm, or it can be critical and nasty, controlling them with power plays and abuse.

The Adult—the person who thinks and acts rationally, without emotion, according to the rules of logic.

The Child—the spontaneous, irrational, and emotional, childlike aspect of the person.

Let's look at a schoolyard situation between Bozo, the bully, and his victim, Jimmy.

"OK, punk, did you bring any money today?"

"No, I didn't."

"Like hell you didn't. Let me see your pockets."

"It's none of your business what I've got in my pockets."

"Listen, stupid, you better do as I say, or you'll be sorry."

Jimmy turns his pockets inside out, and a quarter falls out.

"You didn't have any money, eh? I ought to kick your ass for this. Pick it up and give it to me."

"That's my bus money. How am I going to get home?" (Starts crying, picks up the money and hands it to Bozo.)

"That's your problem, sissy. Get the hell out of here. And you better not tell anybody about this, or you'll be sorry."

Jimmy runs off, walks home that afternoon, and tells his

parents that he lost the money rather than reveal that he has been strong-armed. In this series of power plays, Bozo is coming from his controlling, oppressive Parent which is also called the Enemy, or the Pig Parent. Jimmy's own Pig Parent tells him that he has no power to resist and that he ought to go along. It tells him that he should have hidden the money better and that if he lets people know that he lets himself be shaken down, they will think he is a sissy. Jimmy's Enemy agrees with Bozo—so Jimmy is really overpowered. You can see that Jimmy's scared Child is overpowered by Bozo's and his own Pig Parent.

The Enemy has as its major and only function to Control people, and it is the source of all of the power plays and abuses of power that we are subjected to. Bozo learned this type of behavior from grown-ups around him, especially his parents and teachers who, coming from their Pig Parent or Enemy, abuse their power and control him in the same way.

The Enemy is the controlling ego state in our personality; but as we can see in the example, it doesn't just control others, it also controls us in a similar way. Autonomy, disobedience, and ultimately freedom, depend on not being subject to the influence of the Enemy—externally or internally. It means that we do not use our Enemy, our faculty to Control, against ourselves or let others use it against us. When someone else attempts to Control us it means that there is no strong internal tendency to go along, no automatic, reflex, submissive response. There also is no strong tendency to control others as a way to satisfy our needs or desires. For a more detailed description of how the Pig Parent develops, see *Scripts People Live.*

How the Enemy Operates

There are two ways in which the Enemy ego state functions in the world. Externally, when we apply it to others, it manifests itself in the form of power plays. Internally, it manifests itself as voices in our heads. The Enemy is a reality in everyone's life. However, the extent to which the Enemy operates varies greatly from person to person. Generally speaking, the Enemy inhibits us from doing what we would otherwise do.

There are certain selfish behaviors which are considered immoral, such as lying, theft, violence, which we do not do out of a sense of ethical values. There are certain foolish things which we don't do because they are ineffective or self-defeating, such as drinking and driving, overeating, walking in the cold without clothes on. There are also a number of things, which are neither selfish nor foolish, which we don't do because we are ashamed, afraid, or unwilling to stick our necks out. One of the techniques of the Enemy is to justify its inhibiting commands to us on the basis of morality or rationality, when in fact neither is really the basis of its operation. Usually the Enemy's reasoning has to do with respect for authority. The Enemy is an agency within ourselves of others, outside of us, who want to control us. When the Enemy tells us what to do and what not to do, it is not looking out for us but it is a goon, a bully who represents the wishes of others who do not necessarily have our interests in mind at all.

The Pig Parent keeps us in line and obedient to authority, by making us feel not-OK, by convincing us that we are bad, stupid, crazy, ugly, or sick, and that therefore anything we believe in or anything we feel is not valid unless it has the approval of those whom we respect and who have authority over us. In some people's awareness, the Enemy is an insistent, nagging voice telling them that they are evil and wrong and that they are bound to fail. The Enemy can appear as a rational-sounding, sedate, moderate, occasional statement which undercuts every major decision. It can sound like a paternal, authoritarian, moralistic voice which threatens us with hellfire and brimstone. The Enemy can operate in the form of physical aches and pains, nightmares, or white-hot flashes of dread. Most of us are aware of voices in our heads which tell what is wrong with us and how what we're doing is wrong. If people are lying to us and we want to question their statements, the Enemy will tell us that we have no right to ask such questions, that we are arrogant, and presumptuous. If somebody is trying to intimidate us, the Enemy will say that we are weak, we don't have the strength to resist, that no matter what we will do, we will fail. If somebody is trying to take away what is ours, then the Enemy will tell us we don't deserve it, that we didn't work hard enough to earn it, and that it wasn't going to last anyway. If somebody is overpowering us with fast talk and phony arguments, the Pig Parent tells us that we are ignorant, uneducated, haven't read enough, and simply don't know enough to be able to defend ourselves against such abuse.

Not everyone is equally conscious of what the Enemy is actually saying. For some of us, the Enemy's words are crystal clear like a tape recording inside of our minds. Others experience the Enemy as an ominous feeling, a fear of death, which beckons them to submit, to give up, relinquish power, play dead.

In any case, whether through clear-cut verbal messages or vague feelings of dread and despair, the Enemy saps our power to resist and makes us obedient to the abuses of others.

No matter what form the Enemy takes, it cannot survive and be effective if we challenge it. The Enemy continues to operate only because we are willing to countenance it and to accept it as a valid part of our world. In order to defeat it, we need to recognize that it is arbitrary and that it has been handed down from others, has been internalized, and is now being listened to. As long as it is listened to, believed, and followed, then the Enemy has power. It is therefore important to be aware of the operation of the Enemy in ourselves and others and to actively work against it. I provided a detailed description of how to struggle and defeat the Enemy in *Healing Alcoholism* because the Enemy plays a very important role in people's powerlessness *vis-à-vis* drugs and alcohol. In the book I describe step by step the process for pushing it out of our lives; further information about the Enemy and how to deal with it can be found in Robert Schwebel's article "Blaming Ourselves" in *Issues in Cooperation and Power*.

How strong our Enemy is has a lot to do with whether we feel powerful or powerless in our everyday life. Let us now look at the subjective feeling of power.

4

THE SUBJECTIVE FEELING OF POWER

Power is a matter of great interest and concern to people; how to get it, what to do with it, what it looks like, how it operates. People admire and fear, want and reject power.

Power can be seen in two ways. Power can be seen externally; how much money, how many women or men, how many employees or servants, how physically strong, how much land, how large a wardrobe, how many cars, houses, boats, or airplanes. These are the things which we associate with power. They are the easily noticeable attributes which fill the pages of magazines and are clearly and easily portrayed in movies and on TV.

But there is another way of looking at power and it has to do with how we feel. You have experienced waking up on a beautiful morning feeling that everything was going your way, and that life was smiling on you. You didn't have a nickel in the bank, but you were *feeling* like a million dollars. You weren't the arm-wrestling champion of your neighborhood, but somehow, for some reason, you felt strong and powerful. This type of power is not as easily visible to the naked eye as is a brand-new Mercedes in the driveway, but it is very real nonetheless.

Some of us feel that sense of power not as an exception, but as a rule. Some people feel essentially powerless and have an occasional moment of being powerful. And some people feel powerful, with only an occasional powerless feeling. That internal subjective feeling of power is not al-

ways connected with the quantity of money, cars, real estate, connections, employees, or slaves a person has. This
subjective feeling of power, the feeling of being beautiful,
smart, healthy, and good, the feeling of being a winner
rather than a loser, has everything to do with how much
people feel that they are personally able to direct the events
in their lives. A wealthy man who cannot control his drinking, so that every evening he ends up in a drunken stupor,
feels powerless, regardless of everything else. The fabu-
lously successful star who has millions of people at her feet
but cannot obtain the love of one other person feels powerless. The mighty boxing heavyweight champion of the world
who cannot discipline himself to train to hold on to his
championship can feel utterly impotent.

I don't want to give the impression that I believe that
money has nothing to do with how powerful we feel. It most
assuredly does. Rich people tend to be healthier, live longer,
have more fun than poor people, and it would be silly to
claim otherwise. One of the myths which seem to soothe the
powerless of the world is that the rich and the powerful
don't live their lives as fully as the poor. Poor people often
think that the rich are sexless, overworked, worried, and
unhealthy. This is not only not true, but it is also very beneficial to the rich and powerful that the poor believe it; it
causes the powerless to forgive the rich their excesses and
accept their abuses of power.

A person's internal feelings of power or powerlessness
and a person's easily visible external power are not necessarily the same. One can exist without the other. Feelings of
power come from expansion, improvement, forward pro-
gress. If a woman's annual income goes up by a reasonable
amount every year, she feels powerful. If, at the same time,
inflation goes up by even more every year, she may feel
powerless. How much we get of what we want is a crucial
aspect of how powerful we feel. A woman who wants to be a
millionaire by age thirty could feel defeated at age twenty-
nine because she's accumulated only half a million dollars.

A playboy whose aspiration is to have many sexual relationships with a number of women feels powerless when only one woman loves him. Another man would feel powerful if he had a thousand dollars in the bank, or if only that very woman loved *him.* Whether people feel like winners or losers depends less on what they have than on what they want.

These curious facts about power are known to us, but we don't know exactly what to do about them. Most of us assume that the path to feelings of power is, in fact, money, possessions, real estate, employees, status, education and as we attain those we invariably experience, sometimes only briefly, those feelings of power that we seek. But because the experience of power depends on growth, expansion, and forward movement, finding our power merely through the pursuit of material things is likely to frustrate most of us. Why? Because we cannot all have the ever expanding wealth and possessions which would keep us feeling powerful, and so most people feel powerless most of the time. Making our feelings of power dependent on material possessions is likely to fail in giving us the feeling of power for there is a limit to how much we can get. When our feelings of power depend on nonmaterial things such as love, wisdom, passion or the capacity to communicate then our needs for constant expansion and growth can be satisfied because these things are limitlessly available. We can always find another person to love or love one person more, there is always something new to learn about or teach or read about. There is always another issue to get involved in, succeed in communicating about, and be passionately involved in.

The feeling of powerlessness comes from worries of not being able to get the job we want or earn the salary we need for our living expenses and old age security or to obtain the affections of that person we love, of not being able to control our behavior, of not being able to stop smoking or drinking, of not being able to wake up or go to sleep, or not being able to control our temper, or our loving feelings, of not being able to keep our mind on a subject, or to prevent our minds from being terrified, hopeless, or suicidal, of not being able to defend ourselves against unfair treatment or persecution, of not being able to stop our headaches, and backaches, or get over our colds and illnesses. All of these are the common everyday experiences of powerlessness, which the majority of people suffer to some extent. People who are able to successfully do all of the above would clearly be happy and would undoubtedly feel powerful regardless of how rich or influential they were otherwise.

Powerlessness

It's 6:30 in the morning. The alarm goes off. Jack is jolted out of a deep, inert sleep, his heart beating wildly, as he stares at the clock in disbelief. It seems only minutes ago that he finally decided to take a sleeping pill half an hour after the last TV station signed off. He curses thickly as he tries to relax so as to face the day. His body feels leaden and he is worried that, like yesterday, and every working day as far back as he can remember, he will be sleepy all day, and that later, after he gets away from his job and has a couple of drinks, he will, once again, be wide awake until past midnight. Jill is already up fixing coffee in the kitchen. He is irritated that she can get up so easily and senses that she is avoiding him; they have been fighting for the last month and they never seem to find a time or place to make up.

As Jack drifts into a dream, he is reawakened by the snooze alarm. "Have to get up. Late to work again. Not again. Not today." He sits on the edge of the bed and realizes that his head aches and his back is stiff. "Take an aspirin? Better not—coffee will do the trick."

Later, as he sips his saccharined coffee, Jack stares dumbly at some sweet rolls on the table. He's definitely overweight now, and it seems that his feeble efforts at dieting and jogging in order to regain his youthful figure are not working. "Oh, what the hell!" He reaches for a doughnut; at least this way he won't have that sour bellyache that coffee alone gives him for the rest of the morning. After a perfunctory kiss, he runs down the stairs to catch the bus; he'll have to hurry, but he's still on time. As he runs down the street, he slips and almost falls on the wet sidewalk. Half a block down the street, he remembers to check his pockets. "God damn, forgot again!" He turns around, speeds back up the stairs, frantically crashes through the door. "I forgot to get change for the bus." Jill looks disgusted, hands him the petty-cash jar. He quickly grabs some coins and runs out the door again. He's definitely late now, and just as he turns the corner, he hears the hissing of the bus door closing and the loud whine of the diesel engine as it creeps away. "Again— it's happened again! Why can't I be on time?"

Ten minutes to the next bus; he's definitely going to be late to work. He pulls out a cigarette; he had planned not to smoke until at least his first coffee break, but this situation is just too much to bear. He sits down on the bench to regain his breath. "I'd better call up Charlie at work and ask him to cover the first fifteen minutes for me." He reaches into his pocket for a dime and realizes that if he spends a dime for a phone call, he will again be short of change for bus fare. The phone booth is about half a block away from the bus stop; on the way to the booth, he buys a daily paper, which he doesn't really want but it's the only way to get change. There is somebody in the booth making a call. Another wave of frustration washes over him. Is this woman going to let him make his phone call? She looks at him from the corner of her eye and pretends not to see him as she continues her conversation. He places himself in her line of sight, shifts from foot to foot. His anger mounts as she calmly talks on, ignoring his presence. He can barely see the bus stop from where he stands, and he's now considering skipping the phone call to make sure not to miss the bus a second time. After a few nervous minutes, the conversation in the booth is over and the phone is free. He rushes in, puts the dime in the slot, but can't remember the number at work. Is it 673-5251 or 673-5254? He fumbles through his pocket for his wallet. He seems to remember that he wrote the number down on a slip of paper. He finds his wallet and the slip, puts the wallet on the shelf, and dials the number. Luckily, Charlie is right there, answers the phone, and after a short exchange agrees to cover for Jack. Sighing with relief, Jack looks and sees the bus coming at a safe distance. He quickly walks to the stop and is off to work.

At work, he's glad to sink into his chair and get to work. No one seems to have noticed that he was late and at last he can relax. Suddenly a flash of panic strikes him. His hand darts to his pocket. "My wallet—I forgot my fucking wallet in the phone booth." He stands up, furiously patting all of his pockets. He's definitely forgotten his wallet. No doubt about it. A cramp grips his stomach; he drops into his chair in despair. He escapes into the men's room. As he sits on the stool, having the third cigarette of the day, he remembers that he has been constipated now for two weeks, after a two-week bout with the runs. He is utterly despondent; he feels powerless; he's considering suicide. He hates his work, his wife ignores him, he's sick, he's overweight, he smokes and drinks too much, he can't keep up with his debts, and he feels utterly without control over anything in his life. He puts his face in his hands. He wants to cry, but the tears won't come. He stifles a groan.

On the same day, John, Jack's neighbor, had been awake and reading for about half an hour when he realized that he had better get out of bed. He especially enjoys the mornings when he wakes up early and reads or listens to the radio for a few minutes before getting up to go to work. He is wide awake now and thinking ahead with pleasure to this evening, when Mary will be back from her trip to her relatives. They'll put together a tasty meal, and sleeping with Mary is always a wonderful treat. John gets out of bed, stretches, bends, looks at himself in the mirror. "Not bad for a man my age," he thinks. "I'll have to take off a few pounds around the waist, though." He goes to the bathroom, takes a quick shower, shaves, and brushes his teeth, while listening to the weather report. "It's going to be a cold day today; I'd better take a warm coat," he thinks to himself on the way to the kitchen. He pours himself a glass of orange juice while looking at his appointment book. He considers making himself some eggs, decides against it (too fattening). "I have to remember to take my checkbook to work so that I can go shopping at lunchtime," he says to himself. He looks at his watch and sees that he has plenty of time. He reaches for the phone, dials, and Mary's sleepy voice answers. "Good morning. How was your sleep?"

"Fine. Shall I bring something tonight?"

"No, we have everything."

"Okay, see you at five-thirty. Have a good day."

"Oh, Mary—I love you." Grabbing some change on the way out, he dances down the stairs, whistling. Walking on the street, he looks around and takes a deep breath; an early morning shower has cleansed the air, and he notices the birds singing and the spring buds in the trees. He feels light as the air; at one with the sun above the trees, the people in the street, and the earth below him. He arrives at the bus stop a few minutes early and gets on the bus, feeling good because he knows he will have a choice of seats, and smiling at the bus driver who smiles back. Surveying the situation, John picks a seat next to an attractive-looking man whom he recognizes from previous rides to work. Sitting down with pleasure, he thinks, "This is a good beginning for a good day." He takes a deep breath, smiles, and takes up a conversation with his seatmate.

At his desk, as he settles down to work, John realizes that he isn't happy. "I am going to have to change jobs; this job is not getting me what I want." He gets down to his paper work, planning to finish early and begin phone inquiries about other jobs. Later, in the men's room, he runs into Jack and notices how unhappy he looks. John tries to find out what's wrong, but Jack just smiles unhappily. "Oh, just got out of the wrong side of bed; how about you?" They return to work with a friendly good-bye.

Most of us have felt like Jack or John at some time in our lives. Jack and John both happen to work at the same place, making the same salary, and have approximately the same opportunities in life. But Jack, powerless as he feels, could also be a $150,000-a-year executive living on the fancy East Side of New York, and John could be a $15,000-a-year clerk in Pocatello, Idaho. Jack's feelings of powerlessness and John's feelings of power have to do with a lot more than their incomes and their status in the rat race.

I believe that most people gladly settle for a feeling of power and competence, even if it means doing without the external signs of power, wealth, control, and influence. And I believe that most of us look for that feeling where it is hardest to find—in the American Dream—and ignore the sources of power which are based on cooperation: our hearts, bodies, and minds.

What is it in John that gives him that feeling of power if it isn't his money, possessions, and external accessories? Why the difference between John and Jack? Is John just lucky? Is it his upbringing? Was he born that way? If you asked either of them that question, they would probably not really know why.

People don't necessarily understand what leads to a feeling of power and well-being. "Being able to pay off my debts." "Being in love." "Knowing self-defense." "Having an education." "Not having to worry about money." "Getting a better job." These are common answers to the question: "What would give you a feeling of power?" People also know that these are partial answers; that for a sustained feeling of power and well-being, something more profound and thoroughgoing is needed. What it is is not obvious. Words like faith, security, self-acceptance, and love come to mind but fail to satisfy. The answer is complicated and not by any means well understood; what makes us feel satisfyingly and enduringly powerful, why Jack and John feel so different, is a mystery which we will explore in the next chapter.

5

UNDERSTANDING THE MYTHS OF POWER

Physical power is well understood by scientists. It can be measured precisely and computed down to the fraction of an erg—the unit of physical power. The power of engines or the potential for power that is stored in dams, batteries, coiled springs, steam, can all be easily ascertained with the aid of formulas and calculations which any high-school student can learn. Yet human power is not nearly as clear. We know that some people are more powerful than others, and we have some vague ideas of why, but the variables that are responsible for the differences are not easily understood; they cannot be measured or computed.

In physics, we know that power depends on force and the distance over which that force is exerted. This knowledge is probably responsible for the fact that we tend to think of human power in similar terms: that it depends on how far we can push something (or somebody) around.

Before Isaac Newton quantified the laws of motion and developed the science of mechanics, people who were involved with mechanical devices were able to use them only on an intuitive basis—much as most of us still do today. If we have to move a large object like a trunk, we lift up one side, we kick it, we push it about, we step back and take a look at it, and we can usually guess how many people, or what kind of equipment it would take to move it to where we want it—though in the process we may throw our backs out.

If the problem is more complicated, our intuitive grasp may break down. What kind of a ramp would be needed to get it on the back of a truck? How long? How thick should the ramp be? Some people's intuitive understanding (sometimes known as "mechanical ability") might reach that far, and some others' won't. However, any person could use measurements and formulas to figure out just exactly how steep, long, and thick a ramp is needed to do the job. The information on how to make these calculations is available, and can be taught and learned because the variables in the area of physical forces and power are known and can be measured.

I believe that in the future, people's power—(other than merely physical)—will be as clearly understood as physical power is today. At the moment, however, the understanding of human power is purely intuitive; some people have an excellent grasp of it, but none understand it on a scientific basis.

Combined with the fact that power is not clearly understood, there are several myths about power which hold very strong sway over people's minds. There are three major power myths:

1. The myth that most people are equally powerful.
2. The myth that people are basically powerless.
3. The myth that people have complete power over their own experiences and destiny.

Myth No. 1. We All Have Equal Power

People in this country believe in the effectiveness of our system of government to distribute power more or less evenly among its citizens. After all, great accumulations of wealth are prevented by antitrust laws, graduated income tax, inheritance taxes. Corporations are accountable to the people and must open their books and must hold stockholders' meetings. Politicians are subjected to public scrutiny regularly, and presidents have a strict limit on campaign spending and can't hold office for more than two terms. All of these mechanisms are examples of the many guarantees we have that prevent any one person or group of people from accumulating excessive power. We know that some people are more powerful than others, but we believe that the differences are not large. After all, we are a democracy where everyone is equal under the law. There may be huge imbalances of power in other countries, but not in ours.

As one highway patrolman once put it to me in response to my clever arguments designed to talk myself out of a ticket, "I'm sorry, Mr. Steiner, but if the chairman of Exxon or the president of the United States drove past me over the speed limit, I would have to give him a ticket just like you. Everyone has the same power in this country. That's what democracy is all about."

As the officer spoke, I realized that he actually believed what he was saying. Many other people do, too. The enormous imbalances of power existing in the United States were truly hidden to him. Had I asked him whether he believed that there exists a power elite that makes most of the major decisions that affect us, he would certainly have hotly denied it. That lesson in the mythology of power cost me sixty dollars (I *was* going rather fast).

Yet there is such a thing as a power elite: a group of men—most of them not elected politicians—who silently affect our lives without any knowledge on our part and who most definitely don't get speeding tickets though they manage to move around very swiftly indeed.

The literature documenting this fact is extensive. Books such as *Power, Inc., The Abuse of Power, The Power Elite, The Power Broker, The Bohemian Grove and Other Retreats, America Inc., Who Owns and Operates the United States,* to name a few, tell in detail who belongs to this group, how it operates, how its members meet, how they make agreements, and how they affect our lives.

These men understand how to bring about desired results in their dealings with others. In their personal relationships, in small-group gatherings, and when dealing with large groups of consumers, voters, opponents, or supporters, they use their knowledge of Control and tend to get their way because they have a grasp of the variables and forces involved in the manipulation of people.

They are called the "power elite" by some, the "ruling class" by others, the "super-rich" by others, and just plain "rich folks" by yet others.

One major gap in our information about the super-powerful is that we tend to think of people who have power and money as one group of folks: the rich. Most of us think in terms of $20,000- to $200,000-a-year salaries, at the very most. But $200,000 a year is nothing to the super-rich. They think nothing of spending for a watch what most of us would not dream of spending for a car, or spend for an auto what you and I spend for a house. You and I may be awed by boxcar figures, but the super-rich are excited only by locomotives. That kind of wealth and power is as hard for you and me to grasp as the value of $1,000 was to understand when we were three years old. The amounts of money (and therefore Control) which the executives of this country's major corporations play with is truly beyond the average person's grasp. Think of this: fewer than 1 percent of all U.S. corporations earn 85 percent of all corporate profits.

Lockheed Corporation is an example. You probably recall that it recently got a $250 million loan by an act of Congress to save it from bankruptcy. But you probably don't know that Lockheed has bribed foreign officials the world over. It spent $5 million on its connection with the Japanese military alone. By falsifying records, Lockheed, with the help of the Air Force, charged the government one billion dollars (one thousand million) in fake expenses. On its C-5A transport plane Lockheed had a $2 billion overrun, which the Pentagon blithely overlooked while continuing to throw defense contracts its way. When courageous men like

Henry Durham and Ernest Fitzgerald tried to blow the whistle on this abuse, they were fired, harassed, and discounted.

In 1974 Lockheed showed an $800 million profit. Did it pay any taxes? Of course not. All the above facts are documented in *Power, Inc.* by Mintz and Cohen.

The point is that men like the men of Lockheed who bribed, cheated, willfully underestimated their contracts, and persecuted their whistle-blowers, were aided by government officials who went along with and ignored their abuses. And all of this at our expense. Do you know how many teachers $1 billion could hire? What would our cities look like if the $2 billion wasted on the C–5A transport were spent on mass transit so that we could go to and from work? What happens to our morale and spirit when men like Fitzgerald and Durham are punished and the super-powerful get away scot-free and pay no taxes to boot? What would happen if we gave a lobbyist $7 million to make sure laws were passed that protected consumers against the abuse of oil companies? What if a solar energy company received a $250 million loan to pursue clean-energy research?

Nothing, you say? There is no point? Things can't be changed? A lot of people feel that way. We will deal with *that* myth after we dispose of the belief that there are no big power differences in our country.

Whether in our country or abroad, behind the Iron Curtain or in front of it, whether in monarchies, democracies, sheikdoms, or fascist countries, the super-powerful behave as if giving power to the people were a silly idea—not to be taken seriously, except in matters of little importance.

An example of the manner in which our most important affairs are run without our advice or consent and to our lasting harm was the Vietnam War. Most of what went on in that period of time was hidden from the American people. But if you were around in the sixties and active in fighting against the Vietnam War, you will know the kind of reaction that those who rule us can unleash on people who determine to interfere with their activity. Millions who did not support the war were grossly deceived. Their sons were sent to die, driven insane, crippled, and forced to become indiscriminate killers. For many years, nothing could be done to stop the process. People's economic and financial resources were appropriated and used for genocide. The few who rebelled against this outrage were persecuted, jailed, beaten, forced into exile, and made the victims of conspiracies aimed at destroying them. The fact that we ultimately had our democratic way on that particular issue has had a powerful effect on us in terms of the awareness of our power. For one thing, people have now learned that it is possible for a few to crystallize the sentiments of the many, and through effective organizing, mobilize masses of people so that they will have a say in matters that affect them. For another, people have learned the power of nonviolence. They have learned how to communicate effectively, how to seek and use information, how to cooperate in coalitions of small groups, and they are acquiring a strong feeling of spiritual quest. All of these are manifestations of power we learned during and since our antiwar struggle.

But let us not think that those who make the major economic and political decisions in the world will let this process continue without putting up a bitter struggle. The ruling class will protect the power that it holds and silently, constantly, expand it whenever and wherever possible. A major struggle has been developing over the past years: the nuclear power issue. The same people who brought us the Vietnam War have been bringing us the nuclear age, and they will fight our efforts to stop them with as much vigor and viciousness as they fought us when we tried to stop Vietnam. The parallels between the two conflicts are evident. Major corporations operate behind the scenes; in this case, General Electric and Westinghouse (who make nuclear-energy-related equipment), the utilities, and the oil companies. Large populations are being endangered; our children are being exposed to disease and early death. Technical and moral mystifications are used as a smoke screen for the economic profit-making issues that are the real motivation for nuclear proliferation.

Our rulers have learned a lesson from the Vietnam conflict: overt violence no longer works in the United States to subdue a popular rebellion. Their major weapon at this time is lying, though some very believable sources will claim that bribery, blackmail, and murder are being used as well. Look at the case of Karen Silkwood, a union organizer at a nuclear industry plant, who died as her car was rammed on the highway while carrying a set of important files (which, incidentally disappeared) to an important nuclear-power hearing. Those who support nuclear power are willing to ignore and invalidate the wishes of the majority; to interfere with the flow of information about what they are doing; to make decisions outside of the democratic process; and to continue to push through, at all costs, a patently disastrous, clearly useless approach to our energy problems.

The coming struggle over nuclear power and weapons will be long and hard. To succeed in our efforts, we will have to become aware of the existence of the power and methods of the super-powerful as well as the power that each one of us has. We will come to better understand how power waxes and wanes, what feeds it and what defeats it, how we get it and how we give it away, and how we can use it together, so that our collected power displaces the power of those who rule us without our consent.

The monopoly on power of the power elite is threatened by any understanding among the people of its existence and methods. To begin to comprehend what the distribution of power really is, how much of it is in other people's hands is a very important step in understanding power and taking our power back from those who hold a surplus. Without an awareness of the super-powerful, we cannot effectively understand our own power: we can't grasp what power we could have, how much power we have given away, and how much power we have failed to develop for ourselves.

Myth No. 2. We Are Powerless

In the course of an ordinary day, there are many frustrations and obstacles which we as private, separate citizens feel completely powerless over. Whether it is a gasoline shortage or a traffic jam, whether we're being driven crazy by the neighbor's children or by our own thoughts run amok, whether we have to wait in long lines at the post office or can't find a job, whether we have our utilities cut off or whether our checks are bouncing like a bushel of Ping-Pong balls on a cement floor, whether we have to tolerate abuse from purse snatchers, shopkeepers, or giant corporations, we are liable to feel that we are completely powerless. At that point, we then tend to blame ourselves and believe that we are not worthy because we quit high school or did not finish college, that we are stupid, that we lack willpower and haven't worked hard enough. We tear ourselves down. We become hopeless. We give up. When we feel this low, we are likely to decide that we are completely powerless, that the cards are totally stacked against us, and that the situation is beyond any remedy. When we get into this state of mind, we are liable to withdraw from other people and become ashamed of our inadequacy; we feel completely powerless.

If we are powerless long enough, the feeling can become second nature. The feeling of hopelessness, of being incapable of changing the situation we are in, is familiar to poor and Third World people living in slums and ghettos. Their experience of hopelessness is constant, crushing, seemingly beyond repair—and, for the most part, justifiably so.

But a similar feeling can be found in all levels of society in the form of fatalism and nihilism: that deeply ingrained belief that nothing can be done to change things and that things will happen regardless of what we do.

Some people are fond of trying to cheer up people who feel totally powerless by saying that everyone has the power to change things if they really want to: voting, writing to their congressman, trying, or praying harder. Such entreaties, aside from being unrealistic, will only make people feel even more powerless by causing them to believe that their plight is their own fault for not trying hard enough. We have been told over and over that people *can* be powerful as separate, single individuals, that we should not need the help of others to be powerful. The truth, however, is that a person alone, beyond a certain point of hopelessness, cannot necessarily pull himself out of the hole by his bootstraps. An infusion of energy will have to come from outside himself. Assuming that he can't count on God's help (if he gets it so much the better), it will have to come from other people. We need each other's help, and there is no dishonor to admitting it—but we are not taught to see that. Our tendency to "go it alone" contributes to our powerlessness and hides how powerful we really can be.

The truth is that powerlessness and isolation go together. Even if we are powerless as individuals, we can become powerful when we get together with others to change things. What people can do when they do organize is truly awesome. Those who make it their business to control others are keenly aware of the power of organized people. That is why such drastic measures are taken in totalitarian countries against allowing gatherings of people (other than sports events, where attention is distracted away from feelings of powerlessness) and against unions and political parties, all of which can provide much feared opportunities for organizing.

The feeling of powerlessness always has a component which is justified and a component which is not (called surplus powerlessness, by Michael Lerner). Granted that we are, to a certain extent, powerless against all the things and people that oppress us, we still have a lot of power to turn things around. Where one person is powerless, eight like-minded people have a chance, twelve may be able to turn things around, and a hundred can move mountains. Just look at what Jesus Christ and his twelve apostles were able to accomplish. How he did it is documented by Jay Haley in *The Power Tactics of Jesus Christ.*

The major antidote to powerlessness is collective action. The myth of powerlessness survives only as long as people don't organize to take power.

Myth No. 3. We Are as Powerful as We Want to Be

Right alongside the myth of powerlessness is another myth which holds that our life is exactly as we want it to be. If we really want to succeed, we will, and whether we do or not depends completely on ourselves. We are in sole control of our destinies; in short, we create our own reality.

I call this notion "The Son of the American Dream" because it is an artifact of the economic and geographic conditions in which we have lived for the last century. The conditions of plenty, which a few were able to easily exploit to their advantage, created the illusion for most North Americans that success and happiness were just a matter of being willing to work hard enough.

The American Dream has been largely an illusion for most of the people of this country. Lately it is becoming even more illusory. Nevertheless, the myth persists. Many of us still believe that we can and will achieve the American Dream just as some of us can and will win the Irish Sweepstakes. The point is that most of us won't. The Son of the American Dream has gained acceptance among the followers of the pop-psychology people in the "human potential" movement. It has been promoted through millions of copies of best-selling books such as *How to Be Your Own Best Friend, Success, Looking Out for No. 1, How to Pull Your Own Strings,* and is one of the central messages of Werner Erhardt's est movement. According to this view, people are completely responsible for themselves. This idea, which has gained such general acceptance, actually has a valid basis: the pursuit of happiness is a realistic endeavor, and a great deal depends on our attitudes and actions. When this point of view becomes distorted into a mindless belief in our absolute power to control our own destiny, it can justifiably be thought of as having become an idiotic notion.

The word "idiot" comes from the Greek *idiotes*—which means a person who stands alone. The idiotic notion, as John Wikse points out in his book *About Possession,* accordingly is the myth of the power of the individual. There are many people who are attempting to live their lives guided by that myth. They try to feel powerful and assume that if they succeed, their subjective feelings of power will correspond to an actual capacity to be powerful in the world. When they don't get what they want, when they fail or get sick, they blame themselves for the failure, thinking they lacked concentration, willpower, or the proper spiritual attitude. The reality is that success or failure in this life depends on more than just what we, in our isolated bubbles, do or think.

People often feel powerful. This feeling can be based on reality, or it can be simply a subjective condition. Even when the feeling of power is subjective, however, it is not necessarily completely illusory. Subjective power is an effective trigger or catalyst for the development of real power. Self-confidence and the power of positive thinking give us a certain amount of real power because they give us faith and hope. They prime the pump for objective power. But to rely on this *feeling* of power as a source of sustained power in the world is a mistake leading to powerlessness. When a whole population accepts this myth, it plays into the hands of those who profit from our impotence; it turns us into idiotic, self-deluded sheep, ready to be fleeced at will.

Why is this myth so attractive? I believe that, like the bottle or the joint or the opium pipe which are resorted to when things get difficult to cope with, this myth helps us temporarily escape the awful feeling of being unable to keep our heads above water. When we fear that we cannot deal with life, it helps to think that through an effort of will, we could—single-handedly—change everything to our advantage and improve our lives. It gives us hope when we feel hopeless. It makes life worth living. Unfortunately, in most cases, it is not a useful myth. True, hope is an important force in people's lives. When we are completely overwhelmed and paralyzed, a ray of hope is capable of giving us that extra boost, that additional burst of energy which may actually get us going again. But hope is a spark, like the fuse on a stick of dynamite. It alone can do very little to move mountains without something that will do the actual moving. To rely on that illusory spark to power our lives is a mistake.

Before we can be truly powerful, the myth that we are the masters of our own reality has to be understood for what it is. The truth is that we are neither completely powerless, nor completely able to create our own reality. The fact lies somewhere in between. At times, under certain circumstances, we can create our own reality. At times, due to certain other circumstances, we are truly powerless. Most of the time we have the power to accomplish certain things and are powerless to accomplish certain others. What we feel is not only up to us, but is also the result of the reality around us.

Whether we achieve success in life is not only the result of how hard we try, but of what opportunities we find on the way, how many people support us in our efforts, what kinds of resources we have available to us, and how much we know about power. The power that we have at any one time depends on what we muster for the situation and how much acceptance the world offers us in response to our efforts. It is, in fact, a 50-50 proposition (or 70-30, or 80-20). Our power depends partially on what we do and partially on what others do in response to it. Neither the myth of powerlessness nor the myth of absolute power makes any sense at all in the real world.

Jack and John Revisited

The difference between Jack and John in the previous chapter is not accidental. Nothing in my description accounts particularly for the difference between them; so let's look behind the scenes and see what might be going on to explain their disparate experiences.

Jack does not communicate with people very well. We see that when given a chance to talk to John about how he feels, Jack declines, preferring to appear to be OK and save face. He feels and his Enemy tells him that he and he alone should deal with his problems and that it is a sign of weakness to "spread them all over town." He also feels a sense of hopelessness that has caused him to give up and stop trying to stay healthy. His Pig Parent has him convinced that he is weak-willed and he doesn't realize that he is a victim of the food, drug, alcohol, and cigarette industries which with their billion-dollar advertising and public-relations campaigns constantly apply successful pressure on him to consume their unhealthy and debilitating products. His Enemy agrees that he is without willpower.

His relationship with Jill is responsible for a large portion of his feelings of powerlessness. He gets very little comfort from it; instead, a lot of energy is expended in hassles which are a series of power plays over who is right and who is wrong, who is to blame, who wins and who loses. He suspects that she doesn't love him anymore, and he is not sure he cares. But that is never discussed between them, so the hassles just continue.

At work the situation is even worse. Jack doesn't enjoy his job. Consequently his employer is constantly mildly dissatisfied and he shows it by frequent attempts to "boss" and power-play him into doing more and better work. Jack resists with passive power plays. He is often late to work, he dozes at his desk, he takes long coffee breaks and tries to leave work early. Privately Jack believes (again, his Enemy agrees) that he is lazy. He hates his boss—there certainly is no love lost between them—and working in close proximity is extremely uncomfortable for both of them.

Jack has to deal with three major problem areas: His Enemy (which is the source of his desire to "go it alone" in order to save face), his power struggles with his wife, and his poor work situation. All three of these areas are a severe drain of energy and power.

When all the losses are added up, Jack has no energy to spare. He is forgetful. He can't think things through. He has no time for pleasure or beauty. He is exhausted and freaked out at the same time. He uses drugs to deal with his feelings of discomfort, and they work temporarily, but their side effects add to his troubles. Sleeping pills make him groggy during the day. The coffee he drinks and cigarettes he smokes keep him awake at night and cause his diarrhea and stomach upset. To keep his weight down, he "diets," but does it so erratically that he doesn't lose weight, but just incurs dietary insufficiencies. To soothe his aching belly, he cheats with highly sugared foods, doughnuts, candy bars, and soda pop. The sugar gives him a shot in the arm first and causes drowsiness later. Artificial sweeteners and other food additives make him irritable.

No wonder he feels powerless; he can't control what goes on in his head or what he puts in his mouth. His relationships and his emotions seem crazy much of the time.

In contrast, John is more communicative than Jack.

When he feels bad, he is likely to find someone to talk to about it and figure out how to improve things. He and Mary, especially, speak openly to each other and rarely fight. When there is a conflict, they know how to resolve it without power plays, by finding a cooperative solution. At work, though he is not happy with his job, he does his work and doesn't allow his boss to power-play him. His boss is reasonably satisfied and respects him. His co-workers like him and he gets along with them in a friendly, cooperative way. His relationships at work and with Mary energize him rather than sap his power. He therefore has surplus energy with which to watch his diet, exercise, plan ahead, think things through, limit his consumption of coffee, cigarettes, sugar, and pills. He has room in his life to notice beauty and to take it easy, all of which energizes him further. His Pig Parent isn't very strong and seldom affects him very deeply. The net effect of all of this is that he feels powerful.

Let us now look into the workings of power by learning more about Control and people's power plays.

PART TWO:

People's Power Plays

6

ALL OR NOTHING

The fundamental tool of Control is the power play. Power plays are those maneuvers that we use to get what we want from each other. We use power plays instead of asking for what we want because we don't believe that a direct approach would work. We use power plays to get the things which we believe will be difficult to get. There are several families of power plays which will be explored in this section. "All or Nothing" is the first. The law of supply and demand in economics states that the value of something is not only related to a person's need for it, but also to the relative scarcity of it. Thus, certain things that we need very dearly—like water—aren't seen as particularly valuable unless they are scarce. But when something we need becomes scarce, it can suddenly become extremely sought after.

All or Nothing bases its effectiveness on the creation of scarcities. Long ago, people discovered that one way of making money is to gain control over an easily available and needed item, and to withhold it from other people. By creating an artificial scarcity of something that people want, no matter how freely available it may be to begin with, the owner is able to profit greatly. This is the way in which monopoly capitalism operates. An example of this maneuver was the gasoline shortage, which occurred suddenly in the summer of 1975, during which people were begging for gasoline and paid twice the usual price with thanks and a smile. Just as suddenly, as people got used to the new price, the shortage ended, leaving the oil companies with huge windfall profits. Similar artificial shortages have been produced in natural gas, food, textiles, water, raw materials, and in any number of other commodities by simply creating a monopoly which withdrew their availability from people. During those shortages, people seem to lose all semblance of rationality. They buy and hoard these commodities even if they have to pay extremely high prices. The law of supply and demand is so powerful that the government had to pass antimonopoly laws early in this century to protect people from this type of exploitation by enterprising speculators. But people continue to be very vulnerable to artificially created scarcities.

The Stroke Economy

The same economic laws that apply to commodities like water, food, and raw materials apply to certain psychological necessities as well. Strokes are such a necessity-turned-commodity due to artificial scarcity.

A stroke is the unit of social recognition as defined by Eric Berne. A positive stroke is the unit of human affection or love. Babies need strokes to survive physically, and grown-ups, though they can survive without strokes, need them to maintain psychological health. Strokes could be freely available; except for limitations imposed by time, the supply could be virtually limitless.

Yet strokes are in great scarcity because an artificial economy has been imposed on them which reduces their circulation and availability.

This is the result of a set of rules imposed on us from early childhood, which we eventually adopt and pass on to our own children. These rules, which sharply restrict the exchange of strokes between people, are the basis of the Stroke Economy. The rules are:

Don't ask for strokes.

Don't give strokes.

Don't accept strokes you want.

Don't reject strokes you don't want.

Don't give yourself strokes.*

Due to the Stroke Economy rules, something which is very much needed and which could also be freely available—love—has become scarce and therefore valuable, in the same way in which commodities such as food, land, or clean water have become valuable. But water, food, and land are actually scarce since there just isn't enough for everybody who wants them, while strokes are only artificially scarce. Because of this artificial scarcity, people are willing to work long hours, pay money, engage in trade or barter, and go to great lengths to obtain the much-needed strokes. For example: Jack, in our previous example, is getting few strokes from Jill or at work. He misses positive human contact, and he spends quite a lot of money going to bars and drinking in order to relax and be able to have some fun with other bar patrons. He also tends to spend too much money on new clothes and drives an expensively priced car because he feels it adds to his attractiveness. When he smokes, he pictures himself as a rugged cowboy which, he imagines, makes him likable. All of this costs him more money than he can afford and keeps him working at a job he doesn't like.

Many of his fights with Mary start as attempts to get strokes in a roundabout way. For instance, one evening he jokingly referred to Mary as his "big fat Mama." This was actually an attempt to be affectionate, but a clumsy one, which Mary did not appreciate. It was a put-down of himself because he thinks of himself as "fat" and deserving of a

* See *Scripts People Live* for a more extensive description of the Stroke Economy.

"fat" wife; by putting himself down, he thought he would flatter her. His neediness causes him to be confused about strokes, insensitive and rough. He occasionally visits a massage parlor where he pays half a day's pay for a "local" massage and conversation with a prostitute.

Like getting strokes, being right—getting *one's* way—is a common need in people. Often it doesn't even matter to the person what she is right about or what she is getting when she does get her way. What seems to matter is that one's way prevails, is vindicated, is proven valid. People often find themselves arguing for something they slowly realize is incorrect and can't stop, just because they took that position and won't back out of it. In fact, some people feel that once having taken a position, it must be defended regardless of whether it is correct or not because consistency is an important human quality while changing one's mind is a sign of weakness and indecision. This is true especially in politics, but also in childrearing or in any situation in which a person wants to maintain authority over less powerful people.

The need to "be right," regardless of what about, is a source of many power plays and is the best example of an artificial scarcity, since no one is really ever completely right or wrong, everyone is right and everyone is wrong, and any point of view which may be partially correct or incorrect here and now will probably be considered less (or more) correct somewhere else.

Saving face is an aspect of the need to be right and people will go to extremes rather than admit they were wrong.

The last years of the Vietnam War were fought in the effort to save our national face since by then it was the majority opinion that it was a meaningless war that could not be won. Our price was the source of tens of thousands of deaths and endless misery.

The power plays used to "get" these artificially scarce "feeling" commodities (being right, love) are the same ones used to get the *actually* scarce commodities such as food, shelter, and money. The moves are the same, and the mechanism which causes them to succeed is the same though the payoff may be money rather than love.

Greed

Competitiveness and greed are often connected with each other. People who behave in competitive ways are usually only trying to stay with the crowd and not be left behind, not have less than others.

Greed is a complication of competition. It involves accumulating more than we need and more than others have. As an example, at a buffet, a person who is afraid of not getting enough to eat may swoop down on the table and fill his plate with heaping mounds of food. His intention is not necessarily to have more than he needs—to wind up with a surplus—but out of his fear of scarcity, while attempting to be *sure* to have enough, he may take far more than he can use. Once faced with a heaping plate, he may decide that he should eat it, perhaps so that he won't go hungry later. He'll gorge himself and, if he has always been afraid of not having enough food, he will probably eat more than he's comfortable with. This pattern of greed probably affects his eating all the time, causing him to take more than he requires, and eventually causing him to expect and "need" a surplus of food. Consequently, he may be constantly hungry and his fears of scarcity may cause him to be greedy in other areas of his life as well.

By contrast, a person who is confident of having enough might take just a little food from the table, eat it, and if he needs more, take a little more, and not exceed his need. He will probably not stuff himself, and his whole relationship to food will be one of satisfaction in moderation, rather than greed.

The world is full of greedy people; some have a great deal, and some have very little. To some extent, we are all greedy because we all need and go after things that are scarce, and getting scarcer. Greed is one of the most important negative factors affecting our lives at this time—in the world as well as interpersonally.

Greed for money and power is a way of life in our country. To make a million dollars, whether we need it or not, is an acceptable goal which we gladly teach our children. The most institutionalized form of greed is manifested by some profit-making corporations. These corporations are basically legal structures which were originally designed to facilitate the operation of a business by a group of people rather than an individual; they have become mechanisms run exclusively for the purpose of making as much money and gathering as much power as possible. Runaway corporations, such as the weapons, oil, nuclear, and lumber companies, bribe foreign officials, foster scarcity and competition, interfere with the electoral process, evade taxes, and accumulate power, while spending millions on public-relations campaigns to disguise their malfeasance. All of this can happen without actually having any one human being at the controls, so that the corporations are often like machines run amok, made in the greediest of man's images.

Lately, the corporations who have control of the energy sources of this country are exhibiting that kind of boundless greed. Jimmy Carter, a normally restrained man when it comes to business excess, said about them in October 1977, in a brief outburst of frustration: "The oil companies apparently want it all." Later, he stated that they were engaged in the "biggest ripoff in history." The lumber corporations follow close behind, their ultimate purpose seeming to be the ultimate "harvest" and conversion into cold cash of every virgin tree still standing in the world. Neither oil nor lumber companies seriously consider the environmental destruction for which they are responsible. Many of us have been taken in by their multimillion-dollar advertising campaigns. In these campaigns, the Big Lie power play (see page 134) is commonly used; oil and lumber companies present themselves as seriously concerned with environmental issues, when in fact they externally wage war on those who are trying to force them into even the most elementary form of environmental responsibility. Of course, corporations don't need to be greedy and irresponsible. Anyone forming a corporation can include ecological morality, fair treatment of workers, and other values into the corporation's bylaws, so that they can be invoked against the mere accumulation of lucre.

The maneuvers used by the runaway corporations are varied and complex, but one important power play they use is "All or Nothing at All." The message hammered home over and over by them is "If we can't have it all now, you will have nothing at all later. No jobs, no energy, no freedom, no lumber, no ever-expanding economy, no limitless goods and consumption, no American way of life." In the last assertion they may be right, since it seems to be part and parcel of the American way of life—as it has become perverted by our corporations—to let them have it all, while leaving nothing at all to the rest of us.

"All or Nothing" is a power play of greed and selfishness, and is played at all levels by corporations, bosses, workers, husbands, wives, parents, and children, everywhere. It preys upon people's greed and fears of scarcity.

In order to be successful, a power play has to take advantage of another person's weakness. Crude power plays take advantage of physical weakness: the fact that the other person is smaller, less strong, less quick, or in some other way physically unable to resist the crude use of force. Most of the power plays I will be discussing here prey on the psychological weaknesses of people. "All or Nothing" relies, for its effectiveness, on arousing in people the fear of losing something that they have or expect to get.

Again, we use power plays when we want something from another person, and we assume—rightly or wrongly—that it isn't freely available to us. The kinds of things we want from other people vary greatly. We may want material things, such as space, food, money, shelter, firewood, or gasoline; or we may want very real, but intangible things, such as affection, strokes, being right, feeling powerful, or just getting our way. Accordingly, the power play "All or Nothing" can be seen in many forms, depending on who plays it and for what scarce commodity.

Children and some grown-ups play "I'm Taking My Marbles" (or Football, or Bicycle) hoping to get their way by taking away much-wanted toys. "Ain't Budgin" is another form of "All of Nothing," where, in order to obtain more freedom over his own actions, a child will cease to cooperate by refusing to move, listen, dress, undress, wash, go to sleep, stay in his room, or otherwise budge from dead center, thumb firmly implanted in mouth and ready to fly into a tantrum.

"The Incredible Sulk" is another version of "All or Nothing" in which the Sulk withdraws strokes to get what is wanted and is a favorite power play around the house. "If I don't get what I want, I'm not giving nothing." The Sulk will be usually seen in corners or other prominent spots where she hopes her withdrawal is more likely to be noticed. In retaliation, the target of the "Sulk" can play "Have It Your Way" and even more completely withdraw his attention from the "Sulk." "Have It Your Way" is a power play used to react to a power play in which we overdo what we are being manipulated to do in such a way as to cause the manipulator to regret his manipulation. The complexity of the previous sentence is typical of the complexities of people's everyday power moves and countermoves.

In any event, completely ignoring the "Sulk," spending five hours doing dishes after being power-played into doing them, moving at a turtle's pace after being browbeaten into slowing down, or leaving the house for two weeks after being asked for some breathing space are all examples of a "passive" power play called "Have It Your Way," used to counter other power plays. Passive power plays are a classification of power plays to be looked into later.

Power Plays and Games

"Have It Your Way" is related to "Now, Are You Satisfied?" in which a person being pushed around or rushed destroys something and gets away with it guilt-free. Consider this complicated situation: After ignoring his wife's back-seat driving, Charlie finds himself axle-deep in a muddy ditch.

"OK, I admit I'm lost. Now are you satisfied?"

Students of Transactional Analysis and the games that people play will notice that this power play is very similar to the game that Eric Berne called "Schlemiel." [3]* Let me take this opportunity to briefly contrast games and power plays. Both games and power plays are defined as a transaction or series of transactions with a motive and a payoff. In games, the motive is to get strokes (biological advantage), to structure time (social advantage), and to assert a point of view which one holds about oneself (existential advantage). Schlemiel is a game in which a person, at a gathering, makes one mess after another while continually apologizing to the victims of his clumsiness and obtaining forgiveness for his mistakes. According to game theory, the game is played (a) in order to obtain strokes (positive recognition in the form of forgiveness—or negative recognition in the form of anger), (b) in order to fill the time with an interesting activity, and (c) in order to reaffirm what he believes about himself: that he is a clumsy but forgivable sort of fellow.

In power plays, the motive is to obtain something from someone against that person's will. "Now, Are You Satisfied" (NAYS) is a power play to obtain righteousness. "See, I was right and you were wrong. I did it the way you wanted, and look what happened."

Schlemiel and NAYS are very similar to each other in that they both have strokes as an intended payoff. It probably could be argued that a game is a subtle power play for strokes. If that turns out to be the case, then game playing

---

* Numbers in superscript refer to entries in the Bibliography.

will be yet another of the ill consequences of the misuse of Control power. Certainly Berne was aware of the way in which people manipulate each other transactionally. He describes the *angular transaction* in which a salesperson deliberately taunts the customer's Child into buying something while pretending to be speaking from Adult to Adult.

Salesperson: "This washer is the best, Mr. Smith, but it's too much money."

Mr. Smith: "I'll buy it." (Nobody tells me what I can't afford!)

"All or Nothing" is a power play used by workers when they strike and collectively decide to withdraw their labor in order to get concessions from management. "I resign" is used by some people who have reason to believe that their services are important enough that to threaten to withdraw them would cause the boss to give in on some point. Robert Moses, the power broker of New York City, and Henry Kissinger, both experts on the use of power, were masters of this maneuver.

Both of them got a great deal of what they wanted in that way. "I resign" when used as "All or Nothing" shows how the power play is basically a bluff. It uses the fear of loss of everything to stop people from asking for what they want. Nelson Rockefeller finally rendered Moses powerless by accepting his resignation. Unhappily, Kissinger was never taken up on his offers.

In relationships between men and women, "All or Nothing" is often played in the form of "Move In or Move On," "Love Me or Leave Me," and "Fish or Cut Bait" by a person who wants a commitment from another. This can be effective in getting men to "take the plunge" when they are reluctant to get involved. When women use "All or Nothing," they are usually trying to obtain security (the payoff). They are trying to create a scarcity of emotional warmth and sexuality. When men use it, they are often after sex (the payoff), and threatening to make their physical presence and support scarce.

"Now or Never," "Take It or Leave It," "You Are Either for Me or Against Me" are further variations of "All or Nothing."

Other examples:

Employer: "If you can't be to work on Sunday, don't bother coming Monday." (Do as I say or lose your job.)

Spouse: "OK, let's get a separation, but if you leave this house, you aren't coming back." (If you leave me, I'll take everything.)

Lumber Company: "If we can't cut all these redwoods, our workers will lose their jobs." (If we can't do as we please, we'll create an employment crisis.)

Psychotherapist: "You are free to stop therapy anytime. This is your prerogative, but you realize, of course, that I have a waiting list; if you want to resume therapy later, you'll have to wait until your turn." (Stay in therapy or face the cruel world alone.)

Nuclear-power lobby: "If you don't let us use nuclear power now, we'll run out of power later." (Give in or the bogeyman will get you.)

In the world of business, "All or Nothing" is often used as a technique to bring about a sale. People are willing to work, fight, and struggle for something that they feel is scarce. In fact, as something becomes scarce, we tend to want it even if we didn't to begin with. Consequently, a lot of selling techniques are predicated on creating an artificial sense of scarcity of the item. "The price is going up tomorrow," "Limited offer," "Sale ends February twenty-eighth," "That's the last one in stock" are often used ploys to increase sales.

For instance, if you see stacks of boxes of a certain kind of toaster you want, at a sale you know will last through the week, you won't feel pressure to buy it. You'll be able to decide whether you want the toaster based strictly on its actual value to you. But if, on the other hand, you see only three left, two of which are being eyed by other customers, you might be easily provoked into taking the last one, regardless of how much actual value it holds for you. Its real value will be distorted by the power play and won't become obvious until you get home and you are too embarrassed to return it, or because you used it a couple of times so it can't be returned at all. Often, one-of-a-kind-last-chance-to-buy items are on sale and can't be returned anyway. How many garments which you bought on sale and only used once have *you* got hanging in your closet?

Antithesis

Every power play has an antithesis: a tactical procedure which can be used to neutralize it. There is a difference between disarming a power play, and overpowering it with another, more powerful one. The antithesis is not an escalation of the power maneuvers, but neutralization of an attempt to control. The antithesis is a form of verbal martial art which like Aikido teaches only defense and knows of no offensive moves. "All or Nothing," the effective antithesis is based on being able and willing to give up the commodity that is being made scarce. "I like your football, security, love, job, salary, but I don't need it *that* much" is the most effective way of stopping the "All or Nothing" power play. If said convincingly, it will have the effect of collapsing the competitive strategy and of clearing the ground for a cooperative negotiation over what is wanted.

One of the most extreme examples of that antithesis is seen in the Hindu yogis who, in an environment in which food, shelter, and material goods are extremely scarce, keep themselves aloof from earthly pressures by learning to live on essentially nothing. A little less dramatic, but just as effective, way of dealing with the artificial scarcity which surrounds us is the large movement toward "voluntary simplicity"—or lowered expectations—which is sweeping this country: The slogans of this movement are "Small is beautiful" and "Less is more." "Simple living and high thinking."

People who subscribe to this approach are discovering a whole new kind of pleasure and an improvement in the quality of life when they practice economy and conservation and learn to appreciate old, recycled, inexpensive, home-made consumer items. Of course, the same pressure-selling techniques can be and are used in selling "counterculture," "back to the earth," and secondhand consumer items, and there are signs that a certain aspect of the voluntary simplicity movement is becoming just another consumer fad being used to separate suckers from their money.

Having once said, "I don't need the car, marbles, your love, etc.," the situation is cleared for whatever reasonable give-and-take can occur, with neither of the two parties attempting to control the other person's decision. The antithesis to "All or Nothing" is most effective when the scarcity is artificial—either psychological, as in the scarcity of strokes, or in the case of scarcity created by monopoly. Controlling our needs for the artificially scarce commodity will almost automatically make it more available. This has happened in the case of foods—especially foods with no nutritional value like sugar and coffee—where an effort to drive the prices up was followed by a decrease in consumption and a consequent drop in price. It functions similarly where not needing strokes, or security, or sex from any one person tends to deflate the "All or Nothing" power play and make strokes, security, or sex more available.

Unfortunately, the antithesis may not work as well when certain important scarcities are concerned. The proper antithesis is not a bluff (which is just a counter-power play) but a genuine detachment from what we once needed. It is hard to detach oneself from things like basic foods, shelter, and jobs, and when people power play us in these areas, we may need to fight back with power plays of our own if necessary to obtain our due. The mere existence of unions and other political power groups are effective in discouraging the "All or Nothing" power plays of corporations and other powerful institutions. By their implicit and real support of people's resistance, they reduce the fear of scarcity which causes people to let themselves be manipulated.

When the "All or Nothing" becomes "All or Death" as it did in Hitler's Germany, where not to go along completely meant almost certain imprisonment and probable death, the antithesis becomes very difficult since it requires not caring about remaining alive ("I like to live, but I don't need it").

Antithesis vs. Escalation

To illustrate the distinction between a retaliatory power play, which only prolongs the competitive situation, and an antithesis, let's say that you have found a car that you like at a used-car lot. A salesman has noticed your interest, you've asked how much the car sells for, and he's given you the price of $3,700. You have said that you like the car but the price is too high, and that you would like to buy the car for less, so you'll try other lots.

Salesman: "Well, I think it is a fine idea that you should go and check other prices, but I want you to know that there is a lady who just went home to see if she could get the money together to buy the car ("Buy now, it will be gone later"). But feel free to shop around. If we sell this one there will be others."

Let's say that you are not so attached to the car (though you still want it) that you are impervious to this power play; you see right through it. You now have two choices. One is to power-play the salesman back and say, "Well, certainly if there's someone who wants to buy the car, it seems to me she should go right ahead and have it, so I guess I won't bother coming back." (Have It Your Way.) You are turning the tables on the salesman and giving him some of his own medicine. The other alternative is to ignore his move, smile, and say, "Well, I'll take my chances ("I like the car, but I don't need it"). I think I will go and shop around and see what else is available. I might be back, though. Thank you for your help."

I am not predicting which of these two approaches will get you a cheaper price for the car. It could well be that turning the tables and power-playing the salesman will be effective, although I think it is generally foolish to think that an amateur like you could ever get the upper hand on a professional. It's more likely that he will use a series of sub-maneuvers which you're *not* aware of, and that, in the end, he will power-play you into paying a larger price than you needed to pay. I'm using this example only to contrast the two alternatives that people have when they are power-played: the antithesis, which is a neutralization of the power play, or escalation, the competitive countermove, which, in effect, continues the war.

The question always comes back: When is it legitimate to "go to war"—to power-play back? Some pure pacifists will say, "Never!" Others will say that in order to fight oppression, war is justified. My own preference is to avoid war as long as any antithesis will work. In most situations, power plays can be neutralized; the decision to "go to war" even in a used-car lot is a serious one and should be made with solemn reflection. Fortunately, in most situations for most of us, the choice is not necessary. Knowing power plays and their antitheses can go a long way to get us what is our due. I prefer to study Control-power and its abuses and to develop nonviolent methods of dealing with it, while hoping that no one will escalate their efforts to control me and those I love to the point that war is necessary. Above all, I like to approach every situation in a peaceful and cooperative manner, rather than on a competitive, warlike footing; in the end, I have noticed, I get more of what I want that way and so does everybody else. Marshall Rosenberg's excellent book *From Now On* explores the nonviolent approach to conflict for people who want to pursue it in detail.

This is true in almost every situation, except where our

competitor has ruthlessly determined to take all at all costs. In this case, war is the only response that will work to keep what is ours.

The Cooperative Solution

The cooperative solution to a competitive situation requires more commitment and creativity than either escalation or antithesis. It goes beyond self-defense, but seeks to find a common ground of need which both parties can satisfy. That common ground may or may not be possible to find. In a zero-sum game, for instance, no such common ground exists. A zero-sum situation, by definition, is a situation where, if I win you *must* lose or vice versa; what I win (or lose) added to what you lose (or win) always is equal to a big fat zero. For example: If I bet you $5 and you win, my gain (+$5) and your loss (-$5) added together equal zero. Such situations exist in real life, but not as often as we have been led to believe. For instance, if there are two of us in an airplane and only one parachute, it is reasonable to say that in the event of having to bail out, I lose if you win. Still, I could win by letting you have the chute, being a hero, and getting a posthumous medal. And you could win by being alive—or lose by feeling guilty for the rest of your life. It all depends on what is being added up, won or lost.

If all that is at stake is money, then every situation will be zero-sum, which is why in a money-minded society we tend to see everything in that light. But money is seldom all that is at stake between most people—except in the sewers of industry and commerce. In every other area of human need, your gain need not be my loss.

For instance, in the case of the car salesman above, money is the bottom line. You are buying the car as is: no guarantee, no frills. Your success in paying less is the salesman's failure to make more. Period. But let's say you are selling the car to a neighbor. You want to be able to face that person, borrow a cup of sugar (or the car, if it is still running) at some time. In the future, you might trade or sell him something else, and you want a neighborly feeling to prevail between you. You want to be fair and enjoy the good feeling that comes from acting in a principled way.

The exact amount changing hands is not all there is to this transaction. If a fair deal is made, you both win because he now has a good car, you have a tidy sum of money, and you have each other's esteem as well. Mutual esteem can generate future gifts, favors, exchanges, barters which are worth, even if only money is counted, a great deal more than the few extra dollars you might power-play out of your neighbor.

Given this cooperative attitude, what is the response to an "All or Nothing" power play?

Neighbor: "I'll give you $2,400—take it or leave it." (All or Nothing)

You can escalate: "I am not going to waste my time with absurd offers. Let me know when you are ready to make a deal. This car is worth $3,400 at a car lot" (escalation, with a lie power play).

Or you can use an antithesis: "Well, that's OK, I'll pass. Let me know if you change your mind."

Notice that the latter response doesn't accept the power play and proceeds to seek a cooperative dialogue without the pressures and fears of scarcity.

7

INTIMIDATION

Before investigating the next family of Control power plays
—Intimidation—it might be useful to define power plays a
little more rigorously.

**Definition. A Control power play is a conscious transaction
or series of transactions in which one person attempts to
control another's behavior.***

1. *All power plays are a transaction or series of transactions.* I use the word "transaction," which comes from
Eric Berne's transactional analysis, because power plays are
social events, and, I believe, no current, social-psychological
theory is better suited for the simple analysis of the mo-
ment-by-moment interactions between people than transactional analysis. A transaction is defined as the unit of social
intercourse. All power plays can be analyzed in terms of
these specific, discrete, interpersonal events called transactions. Every transaction consists of a stimulus and a response. The stimulus of the power play is called the power
move, and is the attempt by a person to exercise control in
the situation. The response to a power move can be (a)
acquiescence, or (b) countermove, or (c) antithesis, or (d)
cooperative response. Acquiescence and countermove are

* Even though the proper label is Control power play, I will henceforth speak of it
as simply a power play to make reading easier.

both competitive responses which reinforce and perpetuate the Control-power mode of transacting. Acquiescence is a submissive one-down response which completes the power play by letting the power play succeed. The countermove is a dominant one-up escalation response which becomes a stimulus for a second round of moves. The antithesis is a self-defensive response which, while not competitive, remains in the Control mode. The power player is still seen as an antagonist.

The cooperative response shifts from the Control mode to the cooperative mode; it's neither a defensive nor offensive maneuver. The power player is seen as a potential ally with whom we want to cooperate. Example:

Landlord (power move): "You owe me two months' rent. If you don't pay, you'll be evicted."

Tenant response (acquiescence): "I'll get my checkbook."

Or, tenant response (escalation): "Go ahead. If you try to evict me, I won't pay anyway. I'll take you for six months, and when I move, I'll mess up your house, too."

The stimulus is a power move; the response is a power countermove, which may successfully intimidate the landlord into submission.

Landlord response (acquiescence): "Well, just make sure you pay soon. . . ."

Or the landlord can escalate again:

Landlord response (escalation): "Is that right? Don't be walking any dark alleys if you do. . . ."

The antithesis, rather than the power move, to the original stimulus might go like this:

Landlord (power move): "If you don't pay, you'll be evicted."

Tenant response (antithesis): "I'm not worried about being evicted. I'll have the money next Monday."

Or, tenant response (cooperative): "No need to talk of eviction. I want to pay the rent, but haven't got the money right now. Can you wait until Monday? I'll have the money then, and if you want, I'll pay you interest for my back rent."

This response is neither a submission to the power move nor an escalation. It takes the transaction out of the competition-Control mode and into a cooperative mode.

2. *A power play is a conscious transaction.* The maneuvers we use to coerce others to do what they would not otherwise do are conscious on our part. Sometimes we are so used to getting what we want through the use of power plays that we stop paying close attention to our behavior. People in positions of power are often so singularly successful in getting their way that power plays become second nature to them. That doesn't mean that they're not aware or capable of being aware of the controlling intentions of their transactions. I emphasize the conscious intent of a person in the definition of power plays because in many instances it is not possible to tell whether a transactional stimulus is a power move just by looking at it. A transactional stimulus is a power move only if it is intended to coerce another person.

Consider the following example:

Jack: "Let's go to the movies."

Jill: "I'd rather go dancing."

Jack: "Well, I want to go to the movies. Perhaps I should go alone."

Unless we know the intent of Jack's last statement, we really don't know whether it is the beginning of a power play, although it sounds that way. Jack may be trying to coerce or power-play Jill into coming to the movies with him with an "All or Nothing" ultimatum. On the other hand, Jack's intention may not include coercing Jill at all. Perhaps he is willing to let her have the option to come or not, while he simply follows his preference. This would not be a power play. Jill may feel power-played and respond as if she had been coerced, but it may not have been Jack's conscious intention to do so. This is a very important distinction.

Jill will probably find out what Jack's intentions are if she accepts his suggestion.

Jill: "OK, go ahead. I think I'll go dancing with Jane."

If Jack accepts this alternative graciously and without resentment, then his initial transaction probably was not a power move. If it was a power move, he failed in his purpose and he will undoubtedly resent her response, which was a skillful deflection of his attempt to control her.

Again, what is overt and obvious is not of much help in learning what Jack's intentions are. Jack may not show any sign of displeasure and may go off to the movies alone. It may take him days or months before the resentment against her antithesis surfaces. In fact, it may never surface. So, except in the case of very gross power behavior, we can never know for sure whether a certain move was part of a power play.

The fact that, in situations like this, we often can't tell the real intention of another person's moves is important. For instance, Jack may be convinced that Jill's proposal to go dancing with Jane is a power play, so he may respond as follows:

"That's a power play. Don't try that with me."

There are several things wrong with this reaction. First, he really doesn't know whether her response was an escalation to a power play, or whether it was just a creative, cooperative solution to a difficult situation. Second, her reaction was a response to his suggestion, which itself could be seen by her as a power play. Unless they both want to sit down and carefully analyze each statement from the beginning, there is no possible value to his accusation. He might say:

Jack: "That makes me angry. Are you power-playing me?"

When trying to understand other people's behavior toward us, we can make two kinds of mistakes. The first is to think that we're not being power-played when we are, and the second is to think we're power-played when we're not. Most people tend to be oblivious to the ways in which they are being power-played, though they may be aware that something is amiss. They are committing the error of the first kind: "Polyanna." People also commit the error of the second kind—"Paranoia"—they think they are power-played when they're not. When power plays are common everyday events in people's transactions, life can be very confusing indeed. Genuine, open interaction is constantly clouded by covert, subtle deception and manipulation. Later in this book I will discuss how paranoia is dealt with constructively in cooperative relationships.

Jack's last statement would be a good beginning for a cooperative, honest discussion of just what is going on, but unless a discussion of this sort follows, Jack's only choice is to stick to what he wants without trying to control what Jill does.

A power move is a conscious act and needs to be distinguished from an act which seems to be a power move but because it is not *intended* to be controlling is not really a power play.

This discussion may leave you puzzled. How will you ever know whether you are being power-played? The answer is that it doesn't really matter. More important is that you are not made to do what you don't want to do, whether you are being power-played or not. If you suspect that you are being power-played, give the other person the benefit of the doubt and follow your own counsel. It will eventually become obvious what his intention was.

3. *A power play is an attempt by one person to control another.* Jack: (power move) "I'm going to the movies by myself. I probably won't be back until late."

Let's assume that Jack knows that Jill is afraid of staying home alone late at night, and that he hopes that her fear will persuade her to change her mind. He is trying to control her behavior, a definite power move.

Suppose Jill responds as follows:

Jill: "OK, I'll go dancing with Jane and stay overnight."

This may sound like an escalation countermove, but let us assume that Jill's intent is only to protect herself from Jack's control, not to control him back. If so, her behavior is not a power play but an antithesis.

When she says she will stay overnight with Jane, she could be going beyond self-defense by trying to scare Jack out of his power play because she knows he hates to sleep alone. That would be an active escalation rather than an antithesis.

Let's say that Jill reacts by bursting into tears and says:

"O.K. I'm going to bed. Have a good time." Power play or antithesis? It looks like a power move in which Jill is trying to arouse guilt in Jack by her tears and sadness. On the other hand she may be taking care of herself, letting out her feelings, and going to bed to get a good night's sleep.

4. *Power plays can be overt or subtle, physical or psychological.* An overt power play is a transaction or set of transactions in which one person attempts to control another without an attempt to hide the purpose of the power move.

In a subtle power play, the purpose is hidden; in fact, the effectiveness of the move depends on its purpose remaining out of sight. The other dimension along which power plays can be classified is their physicality. Physical power plays, whether overt or subtle, use physical means for their effectiveness; psychological power plays depend on the use of mental means for theirs.

Accordingly, any power play can be analyzed along these two dimensions (overt to subtle, and physical to psychological) and placed in one of four categories. For example, rape is an overt physical power play, while the Power Spot (see page 114) is also physical but subtle. Metaphors are subtle, psychological power plays, and "Now or Never" is an overt psychological maneuver.

I focus most of my attention on subtle power plays because they are the ones that are most common in our lives.

Overt, physical power plays are the least frequent, although they will rear their ugly heads when we successfully resist the subtle ones.

Power plays tend to cascade from the subtle to the crude and from psychological to physical. They are played in succession with the aim of winning and will escalate from subtle psychological to overt physical until one or the other player capitulates. Only very rarely, once the competitive flow begins, does one or both of the people stop and refuse to continue in that vein. Mark, for instance, went from subtle attempts to manipulate Joan, to yelling, clenching his fists, and eventually he even considered rape—the crudest of sexual power plays.

Let us now investigate another major "family" of power plays, Intimidation, which illustrates the escalation from subtle to crude and from psychological to physical. Like "All or Nothing," Intimidation in its crude forms thrives on people's fear; on the subtle side, it exploits people's guilt. On the most physical and crude end is the "Fist in the Face." Not many of those reading this book (mostly white, middle-class, and educated) will have experienced this form of intimidation, but it occurs frequently among poor and working-class people—especially from men to women and also between men. It is a constant threat in the lives of all women who live in North American cities, in the form of rape. It is a constant potential threat to all women relating to men in the form of wife-beating and in the lives of children in the form of corporal punishment. It is pervasive not only in other parts of the world, like South America, but even in certain parts of our country—especially in our inner cities. Certainly, it is part of our past; intimidation through force, torture, rape, kidnapping, beatings, mass imprisonment and mass murder, all part of our ancestral history, and some will say, of our present. They are the historical precursors of all of the other, more subtle Intimidation power plays in this family.

We pride ourselves on being civilized human beings and

would not, under normal circumstances, try to achieve our purposes by threatening a person with violence. However, the veneer of civilization is very thin. Very few of us would hesitate to exploit other people's fears by getting what we want through fast, loud talk, fueled by anger, punctuated by insults or using veiled threats.

Metaphors

The use of the metaphor as a power play is of special interest because it is the most refined and subtle form of verbal intimidation. A metaphor is the use of a word in place of another, in order to suggest a likeness between them. For instance, if I want to accurately portray the feeling of a beautiful spring day, I might say something like "The sun felt like a warm, loving hand that lifted me above the ground, my eyes closed, suspended by the breeze."

The sun is not a hand, and it did not lift me above the ground, but these words somehow convey a feeling which I had, and did it well enough that someone else in reading it might get a similar feeling and understand mine. Metaphors can be used to illustrate and make clear, with a few words, a complicated feeling, or to describe a complex image. When used for noncontrolling purposes, metaphors are poetry. But metaphors can also be used in power behavior to intimidate people.

For instance, Sally is a fifteen-year-old teen-ager, who has a crush on Burt. Sally's father doesn't like Burt. He says, "Burt is a nice enough boy, but he reminds me of a wet dishrag. He has no guts." This metaphor is intended to denigrate Burt in Sally's eyes, and stop her interest in him. If Sally is still listening to her father at all, it will succeed in undercutting her appreciation of Burt even if she overtly protests against it.

John and Mary are married. Frances, an old friend of John's, of whom Mary is very jealous, comes into town and wants to have a coffee date with John. Mary is very upset. She says, "How can you possibly consider seeing Frances? Are you trying to break my heart? If you really loved me, you would never consider stabbing me in the back like this." These metaphors (broken heart, stab in the back) are intended to arouse guilt in John so that he'll change his plans to see Frances.

Political slogans often make use of metaphor to get the point across subtly and without actually having to take responsibility for the message. "Right to Life" (for embryos, forget the rights of women), "Save our Children" (from homosexuals, forget our violence), "Right to Work" (and exploit workers). Most devastating and effective can be a metaphor where it becomes nonverbal in the form of graphics, posters, and cartoons. The evil masters of this art were the Nazis. Through propaganda heavily dosed with metaphors they were able to convince millions of Europeans to look the other way while they massacred the Jews. They accomplished that especially well with posters in which they portrayed rabbis murdering Aryan children, or big-nosed Jewish businessmen sitting on top of large heaps of money. One of the things that we as Americans can be proud of is that during the same period of time, in our efforts to rally people against the Axis, we did not extensively use the evil kind of visual and verbal metaphor that was used by the enemy. And we continued not to use it during the several further Korean and Vietnamese wars.

But, in our daily relationships with each other, the use of the metaphor, and of the verbal power plays, is not uncommon. It needs to be carefully examined by those who wish to exclude control behavior from their lives. Metaphors are fine linguistic devices when used to affirm or describe our positive feelings. They are effective in explaining our own positive and negative feelings. But they should be used with care in the description of people and their actions, especially if we are angry at them, because it is then that we are able to use metaphors to intimidate, rather than just describe. Because they are so subtle, metaphors work below the level of consciousness so that people are affected without really knowing why. After being told that he is a backstabber and heartbreaker in a metaphor power play John feels guilty, hurt, angry, and confused. He wasn't *really* called those awful things but the effects are the same. One of the dangers of the use of metaphors as power plays is that they are so devious and they are likely to provoke uproar and escalation. In all likelihood, John will respond in anger and a fight might result.

Metaphors work because they are an assault on a person's self-esteem. If the person is shaky in his confidence about the validity of his actions and about his worth, he will be flooded by emotions of guilt and doubt which will intimidate him into going along with the power play.

Antithesis: The antithesis to metaphor is rather simple. "Well, Dad, Burt doesn't look like a dishrag to me, nor is he usually wet. I am sure that he has as many yards of guts as you do, give or take a few." Or:

"Look, Mary, I see no knife in your back. I also don't believe your heart is broken. What are you trying to say to me?"

Taking the metaphor literally and pointing out its inaccuracy is an elegant and efficient way of dealing with it. That way it is possible to ignore the subtle manipulation involved, thereby deflecting the power move involved. The trick is to detect and be able to pick apart the metaphor because it is usually very subtle and not readily visible.

For example, just by substituting one word for another, a certain amount of intimidation can occur.

"Johnny, your room needs to be cleaned. Please pick up all your crap before Aunt Tillie comes this weekend."

This very reasonable-sounding statement includes one lone metaphor. The word "crap" has been used to replace "things" or "toys and clothes." It may sound innocent enough, but it denigrates Johnny's things, his room, and Johnny himself. It is intended to get him to clean up by the use of a word heavily laden with anger and judgment. Johnny's proper antithesis would be: "Crap? I don't see any crap. All I see are dirty clothes and my things."

Cooperative Solution: Let us look a little more closely at cooperative solutions. They consist of three parts: (a) an expression of how it feels to be power-played; (b) a brief analysis of the power play; (c) a cooperative alternative.

Accordingly, Johnny would say, "Mom, it hurts my feelings and it makes me angry that you call my things crap; they aren't crap to me. If you want me to clean up, you don't need to insult me and my things. If you just told me that it is really important to you that Aunt Tillie come to a neat house, I would probably clean up before she got here."

The above is a summary of what might be said—not necessarily at once and not necessarily as tersely—but it illustrates the elements of the cooperative response.

The Power Spot

In *Winning Through Intimidation,* Robert Ringer gives an excellent overview of intimidation power plays. In his description of the real estate exploits that preceded his literary enterprises, he covers an impressive range: from using a color photograph of the earth taken from outer space for the cover of his business brochure to arriving to appointments in a rented jet followed by a bevy of typists, he thrills us with his coast-to-coast real estate coups and boxcar-figure profits. Michael Korda, too, in his book *Power,* lets us in on a variety of intimidation power plays, especially those in which people through their physical behavior, clothing, positioning in rooms and offices, manage to cause themselves to loom larger and more intimidating than they are.

If you want to gain some form of control over another person through intimidation, Korda recommends, sit with your back to a large picture window so that your victim has to look into the glare and can't really see your face, while his face is clearly visible to you. At a business lunch, invade your victim's side of the table with your personal possessions or arrive thirty minutes late to appointments. Answer your phone while in the middle of an important conversation, or have people call you on your radiotelephone in your limousine.

In fact, Korda's description of the power games that are played with telephones will give you the most vivid understanding of his grasp of the kinds of maneuvers which people use to intimidate others—ranging from the sublime to the ridiculous.

Korda makes a great deal—and rightly so—out of the relationship between positioning and power. He observes that there are certain places which, when occupied by people, will give them additional Control power over the events around them. These places, which can be called "power spots," take advantage of people's tendencies to be intimidated and cowed. It is easier to intimidate people if you are physically above them, if you are sitting behind the protection of a desk or some other large object, if you are out of the direct line of vision or cannot be easily seen, if you can see more than they can, or if you are surrounded and protected by people who will support you and will come to your defense.

I'm choosing the power spot as the next form of intimidation because in its subtlety, it is second only to the metaphor. It is extremely effective as a means of control, especially because it is virtually impossible to prove that a person is deliberately positioning herself in a way that is designed to achieve Control. Nevertheless, it can be observed easily that certain people will gravitate and secure for themselves positions of Control in almost every situation in which they participate. People who are masters at the use of the power spot for Control purposes will go further and take a controlling power spot only when they recognize that they will need to exercise Control and leave those power spots to others when control issues are not of importance.

Any gathering of people will have power spots. Power spots are the locations from which a person will be best seen and heard by the largest number of people. At a party, Korda points out, a power spot is the place everybody will, eventually, sooner or later gravitate to. You need only stand on that spot to meet everyone.

It helps if the visual and acoustic arrangements of the spot conspire to make it powerful as well. Standing in a corner next to a dramatic sculpture is more powerful than sitting in the middle of the room. In the corner the lines of the floor, ceiling, and walls meet where you are standing. This, together with the sculpture, will almost force people's eyes in your direction. At a meeting around a long table, the head is obviously the power spot. Why? Because from it—unlike any other point on the table, you can see and hear everybody at once. That is why round tables or a circle seating arrangement are more egalitarian methods of meeting; they have no obvious power spots built into the seating scheme and are preferred in cooperative situations.

It is an interesting exercise in Control-power awareness to observe the positioning behavior of people. One way to do that is to evaluate any situation and make a determination of where the power spots are and after having done that see who the people are who occupy them. Conversely, it is possible to determine where the power spots are by seeing where Controlling people position themselves. You can check your perceptions about who is in power and what the power spots are by doing these things independently and cross-checking the results. In any case, it is important to be aware of when and how people use positioning as an attempt to control and manipulate.

Antithesis: Antitheses to positioning power plays are as varied as the different types of positioning maneuvers that exist. However, it is important to be aware of the fact that positioning power plays can only be neutralized through actual changes in position. In fact, it is a feature of power plays that they can only be neutralized with *power parity:* with an application of power that matches the power of the power play itself.

Power Parity

Whether escalation, antithesis, or cooperative response, a power play cannot be stopped without the application of equal power to oppose it. Escalation requires an actual increase in energy. Louder voice, stronger sarcasm, more elaborate maneuver. Antithesis is like a brick wall; it has to stand up under the impact of the power play, though it is not required to push it back. The force of the antithesis is gauged to be precisely enough to stop the power play. If the antithesis is not strong enough, the wall will crumble and the antithesis won't work. If it's too strong, it becomes an escalation. The cooperative solution's power also must match the power play's power. It is an application of power of a different kind; The Other Side of Power. Against the impact of intimidation it uses disobedience, gentleness, loving confrontation, emotional literacy, grounding, communication, transcendence, wisdom, and cooperation, all of which are powerful faculties which used together can defuse the most intense power plays.

Without power parity, trying to stop a power play is like trying to stop a rolling truck; so it is important to know your own power resources when dealing with power plays. Sometimes individuals are just not able to handle certain power plays; in those cases the power of numbers may be the only solution.

Returning now to the power spot; when someone has taken a spot which by its position gives him a measure of control over you, you will be immediately at a disadvantage unless you somehow manage to find a position for yourself which neutralizes his ascendancy. You may try to equalize power through other means, but you still will be at a certain disadvantage because regardless of what you do the other person still has the power spot.

The most effective antithesis to positioning power plays is to ask that the positions occupied by people be changed in some way. If someone is sitting behind a desk, you might ask her whether she will come out in front of it. If someone maneuvers you into their private space when you know an important decision is to be made, it might be possible to ask him to meet you on neutral grounds. This can be done by saying that you are uncomfortable under the particular circumstances and would like to change them. Being totally overt about a maneuver which is so subtle is very disarming. The power player is put in a position of either agreeing with the request or fabricating some reason for not doing so.

"Would you mind meeting at the restaurant instead of your office?"

"That would be okay, but I'd like to be able to answer the phone. I'm expecting an important call."

"Oh, okay. Why don't we meet at the Black Hat? They have phone extensions in the booths."

"That would be fine, but those booths are very uncomfortable on my back. My chair at my desk is the best for me."

"Yes, but your office intimidates me. Let's meet at the Spearmint Lounge. They have really comfortable chairs and phones as well."

"Well, all right."

Of course, in situations in which hierarchies are very strict and taken for granted, this kind of a request will be considered an audacious insult; but in many instances, such requests will work. When such antitheses cannot be used, a person is at a definite disadvantage. She can then use more subtle means, such as standing up, or bringing a chair behind the desk, thereby not being bound by the assigned places. At gatherings, it is possible to ask to trade places with other people, and even to take the power spot oneself by getting there first or to move into it when the person leaves it temporarily.

Men have a built-in positioning advantage over most women which women have to deal with all the time. It is therefore a good idea for women, as a rule, when concerned about their power with respect to a man, to relate in a sitting position. Accordingly, men who want to relate on an equal power basis with women will be conscious of their height and sit down or in some way voluntarily diminish their height. The same is true between grown-ups and children and between certain races (e.g. white and Asiatic). In all of these relationships, the person with the height has a positional advantage.

Cooperative Response and the Creative Solution

The Cooperative Response to any power play is an opportunity for the exercise of creativity. The power player usually presents the victim of the power play with an either/or alternative. This is the result of a tendency on the part of controlling, competitive people to see the world in terms of mutually exclusive categories; one-up or one-down, either-or, black or white. The world as seen by the power player is two-dimensional, with nothing in between. The imposition of such narrow dichotomies on reality is characteristic of the Control mode and does violence to a world which is multi-dimensional, multifaceted, multicolored. There is no such thing as black or white, in the real world; all of the colors in between are just as important. Whenever we are told that we must choose between two or three possible alternatives, it is important to remember that there always is another—not yet perceived—choice, which may have to be created. A creative solution exists for every problem, which provides most of the people with what they want most of the time. Belief in the existence of a potential creative solution requires that we refuse to accept the choices presented by controlling people in their power plays. What seems like a zero-sum situation (I win–You lose) is reappraised, redefined in fact, so that no one needs to lose and everybody can possibly win. The scarcities that underlie the power play can be resolved and people's needs can be taken care of to a satisfactory, if not to the fullest, extent.

Here is a situation which beautifully exemplifies the concept of the Creative Solution.

During a workshop on Cooperation, in which I had discussed the Creative Solution, the following situation arose: I had made arrangements with Josephine, a friend of mine whom I seldom had an opportunity to see, to be driven from the workshop to the nearest airport. During the hour-and-a-half drive, we had planned to talk over old times, and we were both looking forward to the time together with expectation. One of the participants of the workshop, a psychiatrist, had tickets to the West Coast on the same plane as I and had not been able to obtain a ride to the airport, Consequently, he asked Josephine if he could come along. At first she agreed, but in the next few hours she realized that she really did not want him along because he would spoil our plans for an intimate time together, unencumbered by third persons. He felt that, under the circumstances of extreme need on his part, it was unreasonable that she refused to give him a ride. She felt that he was being unreasonable to expect a ride and that he should fend for himself. As part of the workshop's activities, they engaged in a discussion which got stalemated after much power-playing through interruptions, raised voices, "All or Nothing," and "Intimidation."

One of the workshop's participants turned to me and asked, "You say that there is a creative solution to every problem. What do you suggest here, doc?"

The situation seemed hopeless. After all, either he came in the car and interfered with our planned time together, in which case he won and we lost; or we refused to take him along and had it our way, in which case he lost and we won.

Where was there any possible middle ground? I remembered Darca Nicholson's words to me when she first introduced me to the Creative Solution, "Whenever you are presented with a black-and-white choice, refuse to make it. Relax. Sit back and let your faith in people's cooperative nature guide you. Investigate the problem as it is, not as it is being presented; ask questions, look at the problem in the flesh and not in your mind. A Creative Solution will come from a rainbow of options."

"What kind of a car have you got?" I asked Josephine.

"A station wagon."

"How large is it?"

"Honey, it ain't new, but it's big."

"Do you have a radio?"

"Of course. What would I do without a radio?"

"Does it have rear speakers?"

"Yeah, I guess it does."

I turned to the gentleman and asked, "How would you like to lie in the back of the station wagon with the radio turned on while we sit in the front seat? Promise not to peek?"

He beamed; the creative solution was at hand. "Sure, that's great. I'm very tired and would like to sleep anyway." I turned to Josephine and said, "If we put all of the luggage in the back seat, turn on the radio, and he promises not to get up or listen, how do you feel about taking him along?"

She, too, was pleased. "Well, sure. I think that will work. I can live with that."

I'm not saying that every situation has such an elegant creative solution as easily available, but this is a good example of how, if one refuses to accept the Control mode, one can, often amazingly, find a creative middle ground which satisfies most of the people most of the time. I mention this example in the section about the power spot because positioning was a central issue here. Everyone who heard the problem assumed that Stan would naturally have to sit up front in the car. Josephine, a social worker, black, and a woman would naturally retreat to make space for him and be displaced from her position of power as the driver of the car and my friend. Had Stan been a little boy, we would have thought of the solution immediately, but to put Stan in the back of the bus was hard to conceive. Once having conceived of it, it was obviously the correct redefinition of the situation. The narrow, two-dimensional thinking involved was that he would be riding in front with us. After all, he was white, he was a man, he was a powerful psychiatrist. By having him willingly give up that powerful position in front, he got what he wanted. And so did we.

Creative solutions are arrived at through negotiation. Everyone asks for what they want, and with the needs and desires of the people involved and all of the facts in plain view, the factors in the situation are rearranged like the pieces of a puzzle. The pieces don't always fit perfectly, but more often than not they can be arranged in such a way that the picture is one of mutual satisfaction and harmony.

Conversational Intimidation

THOUGHT STOPPERS

Intimidation often occurs in the course of conversations in the form of interruption, talking fast, raising voices, clipped inflections, gesturing, yelling, using strong words or insults. All of these power plays separately or together can be used for the purpose of controlling conversations and their outcomes and they work by disrupting the victim's thinking.

Antithesis: People who are accustomed to being in control will use these devices habitually, and they become second nature. This makes it difficult to stop them even if they have previously agreed to do so. Often these behaviors are so automatic that the power player will sincerely question the extent and frequency with which she makes use of them.

In any case, the antithesis is to nip the power play in the bud. This presents two difficulties. First, catching the power play as it is being used. Second, returning to the conversation without losing its thread. Both are hard because the power play, if effective, will "short circuit" the victim's thinking capacities.

"You interrupted me. Please let me finish. Now where was I? Oh, yes . . ."

Or "You are beginning to talk too fast for me to follow. Would you mind slowing down? Go ahead, I'm listening. . . ."

Or "Please don't raise your voice. I can hear you perfectly well."

Or "The way you're talking is making me very tense. Are you angry? Please relax—you don't need to emphasize what you say quite as much. I'm getting the point."

Or "Your gestures are distracting me. Please try just to say what it is you want to say without using your arms (or pacing around, or jabbing your finger in my chest).

Or "Don't yell. I'm not willing to talk to you if you are going to yell at me."

Or "You said I *always* make a mess and I *never* clean it up. That is a little strong, don't you think? Please don't exaggerate."

Or "I will not have you call me names. I am not an idiot and won't continue this conversation if you don't stop your insults."

Or "You can't pound the table (punch the wall, kick the dog, slam the door) if you expect to talk to me. I won't tolerate it one more time. Please stop and speak to me without all this violence (noise, commotion)."

Cooperative Response: Keeping in mind the formula of (a) self-disclosure of feelings generated by power play; (b) description of behavior involved in the power play; (c) cooperative proposal, let me give an abbreviated example:

"Damn! I am really angry right now. (a) Do you realize

you cut me off in the middle of my sentence? (b) My train of thought was completely interrupted and I'm furious. (a) You do this to me a lot (b) and I have allowed you to do it. I don't want to do it anymore. Can we figure out some way of stopping it?" (c)

Of course this monologue would not work as is. Chances are that the power player will interrupt, talk fast, gesture, and even bang on the table in the process of establishing a cooperative mode of conversation. The ins and outs of working out a satisfactory outcome will be covered in Chapter 11.

YOUGOTTOBEKIDDING

This is an effective, guilt-provoking power play. The power move consists of feigning shocked disbelief that the person is doing what he is doing.

"You don't really believe that, do you, John?"

"Kathy, you don't actually plan to take the car tonight, do you?"

"You didn't actually ask your sister, her three children, and the German shepherds to stay for the weekend, did you, Pat?"

The aim of the power play of course is to get John to disown his beliefs, Kathy to give up the car, or Pat to disinvite her sister.

Antithesis: The antithesis of "Yougottobekidding" is to simply say: "Yes, I believe that," "I am planning on taking the car tonight," and "I invited my sister, just as you said," thereby refusing to respond with guilt or by backing out.

Cooperative Response: "The way you said that it seems that you find what I am doing unbelievable for some reason. My first reaction was to feel guilty but as I think about it, it makes me angry that you seem so amazed. In fact that is what I believe (or plan to do). If you don't like it, I would like to know why and we can talk about what I can do to deal with your displeasure."

LOGIC

Logic is a powerful tool for the search after truth. Given truthful premises, any conclusion that is reached through the appropriate use of logic will be truthful as well. Because of the prestige that logic holds in the minds of people, it can be used to intimidate them.

Logic can be used as a power play by presenting false premises and following appropriate logical rules, or by presenting true premises and using fallacious logic, or by using false premises and false logic. Another form of logic power plays is to discredit someone else's premises or sources.

IF YOU CAN'T PROVE IT, YOU CAN'T DO IT

Mr. and Ms. Smith are planning to go on vacation. Mr. Smith wants to go to the lake and Ms. Smith wants to go to the mountains.

We approach them as they are debating where to go.

Mr. S.: "Going to the mountain doesn't make any sense. Why shouldn't we go to the lake?" (This is an invitation for Ms. Smith to prove that going to the mountain is a better choice. If Ms. Smith falls for it, she will try to prove her point—which of course cannot be proven by any logical means since it is simply a matter of preference.)

Ms. S.: "The mountain is better. It's cheaper, it's healthier, it's more fun."

Mr. S.: "That's totally illogical. First of all, it's farther away, and it costs more to get there. Second of all, there are much better opportunities to exercise at the lake, so it's not healthier. Third, there are many more people and more activities to do by the lake, so it's not even more fun. Therefore, the mountain is not really better. So we'll go to the lake—right?"

Ms. S.: "Well, I guess so. . . ."

Notice the orderly—though illogical—refutation of arguments, followed by a "therefore" just prior to a false conclusion. Because of the orderly approach (First, Second, and Third) and the language of logic, this sounds like a valid argument that refutes her position; the argument sounds vaguely like the arguments we all learned in high schools, "A is bigger than B, B is bigger than C, so A is bigger than C" and the use of the word "therefore" or "so" especially gives the impression that one has just engaged in a logic-tight argument. The problem is: First, that Mr. S's argument does not account for the fact that the hotel at the lake costs twice as much as at the mountains. Second, there are as many opportunities at the mountains for exercise, though perhaps not as many chances to exercise one's beer-drinking elbow. Third, obviously Mr. S. has a different idea of fun than Ms. S. so his arguments don't hold any logical water. Right?

Mr. Smith has overwhelmed Ms. Smith with a series of logical-sounding fallacies, which include the use of the Socratic method, where the mentor patiently leads the student through a series of logical steps to the final, correct conclusion.

One effective device for finishing off a false Socratic argument is to punctuate the end of a string of fallacies with the question, "Right?" which causes the confused student to automatically respond to it by agreeing. This last maneuver is similar to the maneuver used in "Yougottobekidding" where the person is lead to say "Wrong" instead of "Right" in response to the power play.

Antithesis: The antithesis to such logic power plays is to refute the logic involved or to refuse to prove the validity of one's preferences, beliefs or actions.

To the preceding statement by Mr. Smith, Ms. Smith could answer: "Wrong! What you say makes no logical sense, and so your conclusion is incorrect." She can then proceed to pick through every fallacy in his argument or she can offer to write down his argument and check it out with a logician. But a much better way to deal with the power play would be to simply refuse the invitation to prove anything. A preference is a preference. No proof of a preference is needed. Ms. Smith wants to go to the mountains. That's all there is to it. The question here is not whether or not she can *prove* that this is the correct thing to do. The question is simply the right to want something different from that which Mr. Smith wants. If she has that right, then she does not need to prove the validity of her desires.

Cooperative Response: "Your attempt to use logic in this situation confuses me. I am not sure your logic is better than mine. We have a disagreement here, and if we can agree that we both have the right to our preferences, than maybe we can figure out a creative, cooperative solution to our disagreement."

"I have been thinking that going to the seashore might be a good idea—there will be people there for you to hang out with and I can get a little solitude and it won't be as expensive as the lake. What do you think?"

Discrediting Sources

The invalidation of another person's point of view by discrediting the premises on which the point of view is based is another logic power play. Let's say that Mr. Smith is getting concerned with how much sugar the children are eating. He has read in many different sources that refined sugar is harmful to children's health. Ms. Smith claims that the only thing that's wrong with sugar is that it causes cavities, so it is sufficient that the children brush their teeth after every meal. Mr. Smith insists, "Well, I've read that refined sugar is really very bad for you. It's supposed to be addictive, and it causes a whole lot of problems with your metabolism. Plus, it is completely useless as food. I'd like to cut it out of our diet."

Ms. Smith: "You're just reading too much of that conservationist garbage. They're just a bunch of sissy-trouble-makers who are dissatisfied with the American Way of Life." (By discrediting the sources of Mr. Smith's premises, Ms. Smith invalidates his argument and can ignore his wishes that she feed the children less sugar.)

Antithesis: All sources can be discredited. Scientists cheat in their research. Corporations and advertisers lie. The government is made up of the best politicians money can buy, and so on.

What sources one believes is again a matter of preference. Therefore, the antithesis to this type of power play, again, is to point out that we are entitled to our beliefs regardless of what anyone else might think.

"Well, you are entitled to your opinion but I believe sugar is a health hazard and I agree with anyone else who wants to do something about how much sugar people eat."

REDEFINITION

Another way in which logic can be used to overpower others is redefinition. For instance, Johnny wants to stay out past midnight.

Johnny: "Please, Dad. I worked hard all weekend, and I want to go out and have fun with my friends. They're going to the movies, and then we want to go out and eat. I don't want to have to come back before we are all through."

Mr. Smith: "I want you to come home before midnight. You have to go to school tomorrow."

Johnny: "Please, Dad! This is really important to me . . . will you let me stay out?"

Mr. Smith: "The trouble with you is that you're a disobedient troublemaker. Just because you are working part-time, you think you can have anything you want around here! I'm not going to let my son call the shots in this house. I'm still your father, and don't you forget it!"

Johnny (deeply hurt and upset): "That's not true. I try to

do what you ask. The trouble is you are never satisfied. You're the boss all right. You're a fascist!"

Notice that the father has shifted the discussion from one in which Johnny is asking for something to a discussion about obedience, insubordination, and who's the boss, thereby redefining the situation, while throwing in some shouting, gesturing, fast talk, and a few insults for good measure. All Johnny can do now is defend himself from his father's accusations. Meanwhile, his wishes have been completely sidetracked, and he has been provoked into an escalation (insult), which is the purpose of his father's power play.

Redefinition is a power play in which a person refuses to accept the premises of another. Which premises are being used in a discussion is a very important issue, since who defines the premises of a discussion can probably control its outcome. Doctors, parents, teachers, psychotherapists, politicians, and judges usually assume the validity of their premises and assume that everyone else will accept them. When someone refuses to go along, then they are called "rebellious," "insubordinate," "illogical," "hysterical," or "crazy." Redefinition is often a valid refusal to go along with another person's Controlling premises. In a discussion between equals, it is important that the premises for the discussion be the same, and that neither of the two feel free to change the premises without agreement from the other.

Johnny and Susan want to use the family car that evening.

Johnny: "I need the car to go to school."

Susan: "Well, I need the car to go to my women's meeting."

Johnny: "You had the car last time, so I am next. Why should you have it?"

Susan: "We're not discussing who had the car last. We're discussing what is more important, and everybody knows that my meeting is more important than your school.

Just ask Mom." (Susan redefines Johnny's premise to "The car will be used for the more important activity.") This is a very blatant example of redefinition, in which Susan changes the premises of the discussion to suit her needs, expecting to get support from her mother about the importance of the meeting.

Antithesis:

Redefinition is a very subtle power play. Even more than most of the logic power plays, it tends to "blow people's minds"—that is, to temporarily disorganize their thinking and leave them speechless and powerless. Once it is clear that there is a redefinition power play being used, the antithesis consists of insisting on one's premises.

"We never said anything about what is more important. The agreement is that we alternate who gets the car. You had it last time, so I get it next."

Cooperative Response: The cooperative responses to most of the logic power plays are similar to each other. Nevertheless, let me provide one for redefinition. Even though it will seem repetitive, I want to emphasize the importance of this alternative.

"Look, Susan, what you are doing confuses me and makes me angry. You are changing the rules of the game to suit your needs. Our agreement is to alternate who gets the car. If you want to change the rules, we can talk about it. If this is an extra-important meeting, maybe we can negotiate your getting the car this once. But you can't just change the rules. What do you want to do?"

Threats, Assault, Physical Violence

The Intimidation power plays explored so far derive their effectiveness from arousing guilt. As the power plays get more overt and crude, they increasingly exploit people's fears.

The antithesis to threats and assault is to ignore them without fear. (An assault is a threatening gesture.)

The cooperative response to a threat or assault might go like this:

"Don't threaten me. I am not afraid of you. You are making me angry. I'm not going to put up with your violence, but I'm willing to talk about what's bothering you. What's eating you, anyway?"

The most extensive available discussion of options in dealing with crude physical violence is probably in the area of rape. In counseling women on how to deal with sexual attacks, the four kinds of responses to power plays—acquiescence, escalation, antithesis, and cooperative response—apply.

Ideally, every woman would have at her disposal self-defense techniques to neutralize any attacker's attempts. The martial art of Aikido provides a perfect example of an antithesis to a crude physical power play like rape. The attacker's energy is used against him to neutralize his attack. Aikido has no offensive moves, but other martial arts provide for opportunities for escalation so that the attacker is harmed in response.

But it isn't very realistic to expect all or even most women to learn self-defense. Some rape counselors have advised submission as a response to an armed or obviously vicious rapist. Unfortunately, submission ushers in terror, the rapist's most powerful and destructive weapon. The experience of making oneself totally powerless and at the mercy of another's cruelty leaves deep scars upon the soul. To have to make that choice is terrifying, and only one who has experienced it close up can know what it is like. Yet, thousands of women have to make that choice yearly, all over our land.

I am not knowledgeable about rape, so I am not in a position to say what the best option is for a woman in danger of being raped. It does seem that in addition to a knowledge of self-defense, it would be useful to have a knowledge of the options and to attempt to find out the rapist's motivations might be of use in dealing with that all-too-common, horrifying crime of violence against women.

I doubt that it makes practical sense to speak of a cooperative response to an attempt at rape or any other act of wanton violence but it is, conceivably, an option. What it would look like is not clear enough to me to present here.

8

LIES

Lies are a third family of power plays. They exploit people's gullibility and fear of confrontation.

Most people are extremely susceptible to lies, because as a matter of daily routine, we are lied to extensively from our earliest days. One of the most effective ways of controlling other people is by lying to them, and one of the first assumptions we make when we feel superior or one-up to someone else is that we don't have to tell them the truth. Usually, the explanation for not being truthful to those we wish to control is that they aren't grown up or intelligent enough to understand things as they really are; it would hurt them if they knew the truth. Or things are too complicated to be completely explained. These excuses for lying are used by politicians in relation to voters; by management in relation to the workers; by rich people in relation to their servants; and, of course, by parents in relation to their children.

Because of the pervasive lying around us, we take it more or less for granted in our lives. Only in very special relationships, such as when we fall in love, or when our children finally grow up, or when we speak to our therapist or minister, or when we testify under oath, do we feel that we even need to be concerned about being truthful. And usually we have lied so much that, when the time comes to be truthful, we are more or less incapable of doing so.

Most of us know when we are telling a bold-faced lie

because in a bold-faced lie there is a direct contradiction between the content of our consciousness, or what we're thinking, and what we say. But this black-and-white, direct, and conscious contradiction becomes blurred in the other forms of lies that we use in our everyday lives. In fact, the effect of lies upon our consciousness needs to be clearly understood. Lies (our own and others) are corrosive to our minds. More than just blurring our consciousness, they undermine our capacity to be effective in the world. They separate us from reality, create paranoia, invalidate our perceptions, discount our emotions, short-circuit our biocomputer, disorganize our thinking, dull our feelings, and ultimately can drive us mad.

Lies are the single most potent method of defeating people's capacity to understand the world and to be effective in it. Lies about products make us into wasteful suckers of consumerism. Lies about politics make us citizen-sheep. Lies about each other make us incapable of loving and maintaining relationships. Lies about our work make us unproductive and resentful. Lies cause us to go along, to be obedient, and willing to believe that it is our fault we aren't happy and successful.

In order to understand the way in which people control us, and in which we control people, it is important to understand lies in detail.

The Bold-faced Lie and the Big Lie

The conscious, bold-faced lie depends for its effectiveness mostly on the trust—but also on the lack of information—of the person being lied to. You are buying a car from me, and I tell you that it burns one quart of oil every three thousand miles. You look under the hood, and you don't notice that the engine compartment has been recently steam-cleaned and that there is a dark cloud of vapor issuing from the exhaust. The combination of your ignorance and my lie, based on your trust, may cause you to buy this car.

But there is another form of bold-faced lying. It is effective based not only on your ignorance and trust, but on an additional factor: the lie is so enormous that we cannot believe that it can be a lie, even though it does not seem truthful. The Big Lie is a big bold-faced lie. It works because of the fact that when someone tells a big enough lie, we might believe it, even though our senses are clearly telling us that what the person is saying is not true. I once bought a car on precisely this peculiarity of human nature. As I drove it around the block, with the salesman sitting next to me, I noticed that when I put it in second gear, it made a definite, loud grinding noise. I *knew* that this gearbox had a defective second gear. I asked the salesman, "What's wrong with this gearbox?"

He turned to me with a smile, looked me straight in the eye, and said, "All of the Fords of this vintage have this noise in the gearbox. It's normal." This lie was so big that I actually believed it, even though I knew perfectly well that it wasn't true.

The most extensive and successful use of the Big Lie was by Adolf Hitler and the Nazis during the Third Reich, in which the world's populations were manipulated through outrageous bold-faced lies. In *Mein Kampf,* Hitler wrote:

> . . . with the primitive simplicity of their feeling [the broad mass of the people] fall victim more easily to a big lie than to a small one, since they themselves occasionally lie in small matters but they would be ashamed to tell great lies. Such falsehoods will not enter their minds, and they will not be able to imagine others asserting the great boldness of the most infamous representation.

Hitler's lies were the basis for his success. Had he not lied, he would have never come to power. He told huge lies to attain his political goals. For instance, on April 3, 1939, in a top-secret document on Poland, he defined the task of the Wehrmacht "to destroy the Polish armed forces [to which] end a surprise attack is to be aimed and prepared." Less than a month later, in a speech broadcast the world over, he said, "The worst is that now Poland, like Czechoslovakia a year ago, believes, under pressure of a lying international campaign, that it must call up troops although Germany has not called up a single man and had not thought of proceeding in any way against Poland." A few months later, on September 1—the very date which Hitler had set on April 3—the Wehrmacht overran Poland. It wasn't until this point that people began to suspect that Hilter was a monstrous liar. The Germans never did, apparently, while he was alive.

Nazi Germany occurs frequently in this book as an example of the abuse of Control Power. As we will see later, the Nazi period was an instance of Control Power run amok.

A variant of the Big Lie is Super-Honesty. Here a person who intends eventually to achieve something through lying prepares the situation by being extraordinarily honest and making a show of it in the early parts of the relationship. Such a trick is often used by certain repairmen who will fix something and charge a dollar, or nothing at all; or in some other way give the impression that they are extremely candid and honest, only to soak the customer eventually on the third or fourth time around. Such people characteristically use the words "honest" or "truth" or "sincerity."

"Honestly, though, I didn't see any reason to charge anything for such a small item." Or "To tell you the truth, I think you can do better by going and buying this piece wholesale, down the street." Or "I'll tell you sincerely: I am making five percent over wholesale on these." While such expressions don't necessarily mean that the person is dishonest, untruthful, or insincere, at the very least they demonstrate a concern with those issues, and for me, are always a red flag that dishonesty and insincerity and lies may be at the heart of the situation. However, it is important to remember that there are honest and neighborly people who will enjoy giving things and services away from time to time without planning to eventually fleece the recipients of their favors. Such people are deeply shocked by the cynicism they find—especially in big cities like New York or Chicago, where neighborliness and honesty is regarded with suspicion. Unfortunately, the pretense of honesty combined with lies is so prevalent that a truly honest and generous person seems to have become an anomaly.

Lies of Omission, Half-Truths, Secrets

When a person is put on a stand to testify, he is asked to swear that he will tell "the truth, the whole truth, and nothing but the truth." Notice that in addition to covering bold-faced lies (nothing but the truth), there's another clause that enjoins the witness to tell the whole truth, which is to say not to tell only partial truths, and not to omit the truth. Of course, it is much more difficult to determine whether someone else—or even whether we ourselves—are telling the *whole* truth, but it needs to be accepted from the outset that not to tell the whole truth is as much of a lie as telling a bold-faced lie. A lie by omission, or half-truth, is a situation in which we knowingly hold back information which we understand that the other person wants.

Advertisers have developed the habit of lying-by-omission to a science. "Repos can cut your scrubbing time in half, or double your money back." Of course, Repos *can* cut your cleaning time in half, but it may not. It also could, conceivably, double your cleaning time. And there's nothing in the statement that guarantees that it will actually cut your cleaning time in half. The gullibility of the listener is exploited with this half-truth.

The policy about the buying and selling of products in

this country is *"caveat emptor"*—"let the buyer beware." This seems to imply that the seller has no responsibility whatsoever in whatever statements he made before the sale. In fact, we are warned that nothing the seller says should be listened to by a wary buyer because it is understood that it may all be a lie. Unless it is written down as part of the contract of sale, it has no legal significance. Because selling is the proudest and most highly respected activity in our society, we have grown accustomed to accepting lies by omission as a justified and inevitable part of our everyday life.

Coupled with this is the fact that there exists a belief among people that it is good to tell "little white lies" to protect people from the painful truth and that "what we don't know won't hurt us" so that a state of constant half-truth is the usual experience for most of us.

Lies of omission are not as powerful a power play as bold-faced lies, but they can do the work quite effectively. Suppose, again, that you're buying a car which is a bad oil-burner. You ask the salesman, "How is this car on oil?" The salesman can answer, with a bold-faced lie, "It doesn't burn any oil." Or a Big Lie, "It's amazing for a car of this age, and you're going to have trouble believing this, but this car burns less than a quart to five thousand miles." Or, a half-truth, "This car has burned less than a quart in the last three months." (It's been sitting on the lot for the last three months.) Or, an evasion, "It uses detergent thirty-weight." Obviously these lies are decreasingly powerful in their desired effect, but they all work surprisingly well, and it's amazing how far a person can manipulate others through lies of omission.

Antithesis: The antithesis to lies is difficult. No one likes to call someone a liar to his or her face. No matter how sure we are, as Hitler points out, we aren't able to imagine anyone being a conscious liar. Calling someone a liar is a major insult, and we risk anger, retaliation, and abuse. It's easier to just forget the whole thing; it is soothing to believe, and so we go along for the sake of harmony and simplicity.

The antitheses to lies can become involved and complicated. That is another reason why we accept lies. It would be so much easier to believe and act on faith rather than listening to our intuition and taking on the task of smoking out the lie and neutralizing it. The antithesis to lying is, obviously enough, asking questions and checking the answers. Sometimes a series of questions can expose a lie because the answers will contradict each other or because the liar will become flustered. That is what cross-examination in the courtroom is all about. But sometimes in carefully conceived lies, the truth can be found only by independently verifying the statement's truth.

Asking questions is not easy, since they imply mistrust and give the liar an excuse for righteous indignation. Yet it is possible to phrase questions in a relatively inoffensive manner.

For instance:

"I hope you don't mind, Mr. Smith, but can I ask you a few questions?"

"Okay."

"Was the engine compartment of the car steam-cleaned?"

"I don't know."

"Well, it looks like it was. Can we find out?"

"I guess it was. We sometimes do that."

"Why did you do it in this case? Just curious . . . could you find out?"

Or "What is that smoke coming from the exhaust?"

Or "Who owned this car previously? Can I call them?"

Or "How long has the car been sitting here? How do you know whether it burns oil or not?"

In practicing the antithesis against lies, it is important not to be embarrassed to ask as many questions as one has to. If the other person gets upset, it may be necessary to reassure him or her, but the questions should be pursued to the end. A person who lies may use any number of techniques to avoid the antithesis.

Derision: "What's the matter, don't you trust me?" (With a smile.)

Antithesis: "I just want to ask some questions. Do you mind answering them?" (With a smile.)

Distraction: "Yes, the engine compartment and the rest of the car was cleaned inside and out. Isn't it clean? We always sell clean cars."

Antithesis: "I am not concerned with the *rest* of the car. Why was the engine compartment steam-cleaned?"

Humor: "Maybe it was cleaned so you can cook your fried eggs on the engine's head. How do you like your eggs?"

Antithesis: "Over easy, thank you, but I'd rather cook at home. What *was* the reason?"

Red herring: "That reminds me. I just read an article in *Motor* magazine where they said that it's harmful to the wiring to steam-clean engines. Maybe we shouldn't do it anymore. What do you think?"

Antithesis: "Well, if I was trying to get rid of a lot of oil in the cowl, I might steam-clean the engine anyway. Was that the reason?"

Anger: "Are you calling me a liar?"

Antithesis: "No, I am just trying to find out why the engine was steam-cleaned."

It is highly unlikely that a liar will admit a lie. Unlike most antitheses, which usually succeed in stopping the power play, the antithesis to lies tends to increase the intensity of it. The liar can be counted on to heap lie upon lie to avoid telling the truth. In the end, the person who suspects a lie will have to decide for himself what the facts really are. While the antithesis may not stop the lying, it will prevent the manipulation.

Cooperative response: "There is something about what you are telling me which doesn't make sense. It feels wrong.

I am afraid that you aren't being completely truthful. Are you telling me the truth?"

When I have used the above response, it has never succeeded in producing a more honest conversation; people just don't admit to lying. However, it has had the effect of discouraging further lies and fostering more honest communication at a later time.

High Ball/Low Ball

A favorite trick of merchandisers is "High Ball, Low Ball" wherein a person's interest is attracted by a Low Ball which isn't really available—only to be sold a High Ball. Years ago (more than I care to count), a very well advertised and very sexist slogan ran: "Promise her anything, but give her Arpège." Consumer revolt has stopped the most blatant examples of such advertising but it is still a much-used device in a subtler form. Department stores and markets will advertise discounted items in the hope that people will buy regularly priced items as well, and auto dealers advertise the price of their no-frills models, hoping to sell all of the expensive accessories.

When people play High/Low Ball, they make more or less consciously exaggerated offers only to come across with a much diminished final product. "Let's get married and I'll honor and obey forever." Or "Let's have sex and I'll marry you." Or "Lend me your car and I'll tune it up and give you a set of tires." Or "Invest a thousand dollars in my business and we'll be partners."

Antithesis: With High/Low Ball, there are two antitheses possible before and after it's too late. Before it's too late, the antithesis is to make the offer clear by asking a lot of questions, preferably in front of other people, and clarifying the agreement and what precisely the exchange is, in writing if appropriate.

"What do you mean by honor and obey forever?"

Or *"When* will you marry me?"

Or "Who is doing the tune-up and where are you getting the tires?"

Or "Let's draw up the partnership papers."

After it's too late, the only recourse is to ask for what was offered in an assertive way.

"You said you'd tune the car, but it won't start."

"Well, I had the car tuned before the trip, and the tires are new."

"Yes, but you took a trip across the country. You promised to tune the car, and that meant to me that you would return it tuned. Where did you buy these tires, anyway? They are all different."

"I bought them at a wrecking yard. They have a lot of thread on them."

"Well, I want the car tuned *now,* and I want *new* tires, as you said."

"I can't afford that. I spent all my money on the trip."

"I realize you may have no money, but I want a tune-up and new tires, like you promised."

"You are being unreasonable. I'll change the plugs in the car and see if it starts."

"I can understand why you feel I'm being unreasonable, and I don't want you to work on the car. I want a tune-up and new tires."

And so on. But, as I mentioned before, it may be too late. It would have been much better to get the agreement clear before the car was borrowed.

In the above example, the reader may recognize techniques of Systematic Assertive Therapy, a method developed by Manuel J. Smith. This method is a very useful technique for avoiding manipulation. It was published in Smith's book, *When I Say No I Feel Guilty,* which I highly recommend as a practical manual for people who want to avoid being power-played.

Cooperative Response: Again, there are two places in

which to apply a response to High/Low Ball: before and after it's too late.

Before, the cooperative response is much like the antithesis: Get a clear contract. After it might go something like this:

"Look, I am very upset about this. I'm sure you can understand that I want a car that works. I definitely want a professional tune-up. As far as the tires go, the front right and the rear left are matched and look pretty good, so why don't you get two new tires of the same brand?"

"Well, that would be okay, but I can't pay for it now."

"Maybe you can borrow the money for the tune-up and buy the tires on time, but I absolutely need you to do this."

"Can you lend me the money? I'll pay you back next week."

"I'll lend you the money if you sign an I.O.U. and bring me your color TV until you pay."

Statistics

Statistics are another specific way in which it is possible to lie. Statistics can be made up as you go. "Eighty percent of the women in this country are having sex before marriage." (So let's go, honey.)

Or "Ninety-nine percent of the people who we deal with are satisfied customers." (So sign on the dotted line.)

But it isn't necessary to invent statistics. Statistics (valid and false) are available on almost any subject and can be used to advantage. What's worse, special-interest groups often set up whole research programs which are designed to produce statistics that can be used to bolster their point of view. For instance, the Tobacco Institute, which is funded by the tobacco companies, spends millions of dollars a year doing research. Obviously, the research is not done to prove that tobacco is harmful to people. It's hardly likely that tobacco companies would spend millions of dollars with no interest in the outcome of the research. But they rely on the fact that from the hundreds of research outcomes, some of which are valid, and some of which are not, there always are some which could be used to prove that it's safe to smoke cigarettes. For instance one "scientific" statement made by the Tobacco Institute is that there is not yet *conclusive* evidence that cigarettes are harmful to humans. They can say that the *conclusive* experiment can't be performed since it would involve scientific controls impossible to impose on human beings. Only in a concentration camp, could people be randomly selected into two groups and one group forced to smoke while the other was prevented from doing so. The conclusive experiments have been performed on rats, but they supposedly don't count because, according to cigarettes' friends, people are not rats. (Except, perhaps, cigaarette manufacturers.)

Antithesis and Cooperative Response: The antithesis to power-play statistics is similar to the antithesis to logic power plays: checking out their validity or asserting one's point of view regardless of logic or statistics. Therefore the cooperative response follows the same pattern as that used for all the power plays:

"I wish you wouldn't try to convince me with statistics I can't believe. It makes me mad. I told you I don't want to have sex with you, so can't we just be friends? I really love you and am willing to be good to you, but I don't want to get sexy. Come on, cheer up. Let's have some fun!"

Gossip

Gossip is a power play which uses lies for its effectiveness. It is especially effective in close-knit interpersonal situations, groups, and small towns. People can introduce false information in people's minds to manipulate them. A great classic example is Shakespeare's play *Othello,* in which Iago's lies to Othello about his beloved wife eventually lead

Othello to murder her and kill himself. Gossip is a very powerful method of manipulating others and it is extremely difficult to neutralize when a clever liar uses it. Gossip is usually delivered in hushed tones, to suggest that it is confidential information not to be passed on. In fact, it is being spoken to be passed on, but the hushed tones imply that it is not really being said, so that the gossip cannot be held responsible. It is as if the gossip is saying, "I am telling you this, but I am not really telling it to you. So don't quote me, just pass it on."

Gossip and rumors have a way of becoming increasingly distorted and are capable of panicking people. Gossip is used in "disinformation," when in order to confuse people about what is going on, a person plants a confusing, false rumor in a gossip grapevine. It is therefore very important to know how to deal with this power play.

Antithesis: One clever and powerful way of dealing with gossip is the implantation of a counterrumor. If the false rumor is circulating that Jack is deeply in debt and about to go bankrupt, Jack can have Jill plant the rumor that he has recently got a large amount of money and has just paid all his debts. That rumor will join the other one in the grapevine and tend to neutralize it. More concretely, however, in dealing with gossip, questions are, once again, extremely effective. Checking what people supposedly said or did can deflate gossip with surprising swiftness. It is important with gossip not to respect the attempts to keep secrets which usually accompany it.

Jack: "Mary cheated John out of some money."

Bill: "Really? Who did you hear it from?"

Jack: "I heard it from Peter."

Bill: "Who told Peter?"

Jack: "I don't know."

Bill: "Well, that's a pretty serious rumor to be passing around when you don't even know the source. Do you mind if I check this out with Mary and John? They are both good friends, and I'd like to know what is going on."

Jack: "Well, Peter asked me not to mention it to you because he knew it would upset you."

Bill: "In that case, you should not have said it to me, but now that you did, I'd like to find out. Is that okay?"

Cooperative Response: When you hear a rumor, it is very useful to find out its source and whether it is an eyewitness report or hearsay. If hearsay, it is important to know what level hearsay it is. Even if Jack heard the rumor from Peter who heard it from John himself, the information is likely to be hopelessly distorted. Each person who is involved adds his own distortion.

John may have just said to Peter that he made a poor bargain with Mary. He may even be willing to take responsibility without saying so. And he may, in fact, have gotten a very good deal.

John (to Peter): "I didn't get a very good deal when I bought that car from Mary."

Peter then adds on his own twist.

Peter (to Jack): "John says that he got a lousy deal from Mary on that car."

Next Jack adds his two cents ("Mary cheated John") and by this time a nasty rumor has been started. The cooperative response to such statements is to ask whether Jack was an eyewitness to the sale of the car and to inquire about his reasoning for the conclusion.

In general, information which is hearsay should be taken with a large grain of salt especially if it is third or fourth level hearsay.

The cooperative response to a rumor is to check it through to its origin, hear all sides of the story and if the rumor is false, endeavor to set the record straight with all the parties involved. People who make it a habit to follow up on rumors are reasonably immune to gossip power plays because in such a situation gossip tends to backfire against those who start it.

9

PASSIVE POWER PLAYS

Up to now, all of the power plays discussed are used aggressively—that is, by people who are offensively trying to get what they want. But there is a whole group of power plays which are defensive and accomplish their goal passively.

Nobody Upstairs

"Nobody Upstairs" depends on refusing to acknowledge other people's expectations. If you want me to do something and I don't want to do it, I can use a number of ways to talk you out of what you want. But I can also simply refuse to acknowledge the request. "Nobody Upstairs" can be played in many variations. Not listening, reading the newspaper, taking copious notes, looking out the window, or doing something while you are speaking, are good examples. When at work or in business situations, it is possible to answer the phone, or even intentionally have someone call in the middle of a conversation, and then breezily say, "Go ahead, I'm listening. I just have to take care of this little bit of business here."

One form of "Nobody Upstairs" ploy is forgetting or not listening. Missing appointments, forgetting instructions, and in general, playing "stupid" ("Who, Me?"), ("Gee, I'm Sorry") are ways in which one can foil other people's expectations by feigning ignorance of them or never actually taking them in.

Another way to play "Nobody Upstairs" is to ignore unspoken rules. "Golly, I didn't know you weren't supposed to wipe your shoes with the towels." Or "How was I supposed to know that you would expect people to knock before coming into your bedroom?"

A particularly obnoxious version of this power play is ignoring refusals, in which a person continues to ask for something after being repeatedly denied. Women often have that experience with men who will not take "No!" for an answer, and will doggedly pursue their aims by turning totally deaf ears to the woman's lack of interest. Often this kind of power play breaks down the woman's resistance so that she goes along just to get rid of him.

Antithesis: The antithesis to "Nobody Upstairs" is to pretend you are dealing with a retarded child, and patiently draw his attention to the subject matter at hand, making sure that he stays in touch throughout.

"Please stop reading that newspaper and listen to me."

(And later) "Did you get what I said? Can you repeat it to me?"

"I'll be glad to wait until your call is finished. Perhaps we should meet at another time? I'd like to have your undivided attention."

"Are you writing this appointment down? Let me see . . . You wrote it in the wrong date. It's April 16th, not April 19th."

"Would you like me to call you to remind you to bring those papers?"

"No, John, I don't want to just cuddle for a while. If, you don't take your hands off me, I am going to break your . . . No, I'm kidding. Please stop or I'll leave." (With "Nobody Upstairs" players, it is always good to have your own transportation and a place to sleep and eat readily available.)

Cooperative Response: "I am getting really tired and angry when you don't remember what I ask you to do. If you expect me to relate to you, you'll have to do something about hearing me and acting on what I ask of you. How can we get this situation straightened out?"

Notice that in expressing the feelings that are generated, I am mentioning being tired and angry. Often people have a problem saying how they actually *feel.* Instead they evaluate or judge the person. For instance, I am not saying: "I feel that you are not interested in what I say" or "I feel you are power-playing me." Neither of these two sentences express a feeling. Rather, they posit a theory of what is happening; a theory which is not necessarily true and which *doesn't* bring out how I feel, which is tired and angry.

You Owe Me

This is a passive power play which is based on the exploitation of other people's sense of obligation. People who use this maneuver are very tuned into others' guilt. A guilt–power player will set the stage by doing a series of things for the victim all of which are intended to create a sense of obligation which can be later cashed in. Women in need of security from a man will often pave the way by creating the necessary amounts of guilt by being loving, yielding, nurturing. If he accepts these gifts from her, he may feel after a while that not to reciprocate with a commitment would be a betrayal. If his guilt can be hooked, he may get married, start a family, and support his wife and subsequent children for the rest of his life, based on guilt alone.

Conversely, men will use the same ploy on women to obtain what they want—nurturing, warmth, love, and sex— by spending a lot of money on travel, meals and entertainment, with the express purpose of creating a feeling of debt and guilt. When both people engage in these guilt-arousing maneuvers, the situation is even more complicated in that they are both simultaneously power-playing each other for things they do not want to give and winding up hopelessly locked into a complicated network of obligations, bolstered by guilt.

Another form of "You Owe Me" power plays has to do with rights. We are supposedly all born equal, meaning we all have equal rights before the law. But our historical tradition is one in which some people are more equal than others. Some people assume or are given rights in excess of others. It may seem strange to most ears, but not too many years ago, divine rights—the rights that royalty had over the people—were "God-given." The king had the right to demand that his subjects pay their taxes, go to war for him, give up their land, and do any number of things which he desired. If they didn't, they were going against God's wishes and could be coerced by simple, moral arguments (backed by jailing and torture) reminding them of their obligations toward God and the king.

God-given rights were assumed by parents over children, by whites over people of color, by men over women, by rich people over poor people, by "educated people" over the "masses." It is not at all unusual for children, third world people, and the poor to still willingly give up their rights on the basis of guilt. One example is the guilt that people who cannot obtain a job or who are disabled feel when they ask for or accept welfare money. This money is their right to have in a just society. Yet many people will feel extremely guilty about accepting aid, a guilt which is encouraged by the rich in every possible way.

Many people will refuse to accept their rightful due with pride. Pride and guilt are the two sides of the coin with which they are rewarded for going along with those God-given rights. Similarly, employers would like to give their workers the impression that they are owed something for offering them employment. That way they can justify the expectation that their workers produce more than they are being paid for. Often, good workers confuse pride of workmanship—doing a good job—with pride of work place—working for a good boss. They are not the same, and pride of workmanship can keep a worker in a bad job with a bad boss.

Fundamentally, this pride is the pride of obedience, of being a good subject, a good child, a good "nigger," good woman or good man.

"I give you a job, you owe me hard work."

"You owe your life to your country. go and fight. Be a man!"

"I'm your husband; I work hard. I want dinner ready when I come home from work."

"What do you black people want, anyway? Why can't you be satisfied? You have jobs. You're getting into colleges. You can live anywhere you want. Isn't that enough?"

"I'm your father. You owe me some respect. I don't want any backtalk from you."

Divine rights, parental rights, family rights are all lavishly used, even today, as a way of getting what we want from other people.

Antithesis: The antithesis to "You Owe Me" can be difficult. In order not to fall for this kind of power play, a person has to be willing to give up guilt as a guiding emotion. However, giving up guilt as an emotion is dangerously close to refusing to honor obligations to other human beings. We tend to fear that refusing to yield to "You Owe Me" power plays will turn us into people who are callous, insensitive, and totally selfish.

The point, however, is not to become insensitive to other people's needs and wishes. We need to know just *what* we want to do for *whom.* Guilt is not a very good indicator of what our obligations are. A sense of responsibility, based on clear moral guidelines, is a much better basis for deciding what to do than a sense of guilt, which can be easily stimulated by other people's selfish-power plays.

The antithesis to "You Owe Me" then, is to say, "I owe you nothing, unless we made a fair deal and you have performed on your side and I haven't on mine, I have no obligations to you. I'll do what I do out of choice, not out of obligation; so I won't die for my country, cook dinner, be satisfied with this job, keep quiet unless it pleases me to do so."

Cooperative Response: "Wait a minute, Jack. It hurts me and makes me angry that you talk to me this way, telling me that because you work hard and because I am your wife, dinner has to be ready on the table the moment you arrive from work.

"I understand you are tired and hungry and cranky and I would like to help you, but I don't think that I have to or that I owe it to you. I am doing the best I can, but I am afraid that dinner won't always be ready whenever you get here; so let's talk about how we can take care of how you feel when you get home. Maybe you can take a hot shower or maybe . . . (etc.)."

Notice that after saying how she feels, Jill repeats to Jack what he does to cause her feelings. She doesn't say "You are a chauvinist pig" or "You are power-playing me" or "You are unreasonable," but she explains, as closely as she can, what he does that bothers her, without judgment or interpretation, and how she feels when she is exposed to his behavior.

10

THE CONTROLLING PERSON

People who are singularly invested in Control power plays often dominate their environment with the physical aspects of their person: their movements, their voice, their smells. But equally often their domination is much more subtle. It can be perceived only by the subtle oppressive energy transmitted in their language and demeanor, and the long-range effects of relating to them: that we repeatedly wind up the loser, one down, feeling somehow not-OK. People who are primarily invested in being powerful through Control power are seen as aggressive, competitive, ambitious, focused. When a person is all of these, he is regarded with ambivalence; he is admired and envied, respected and feared, loved and hated by most people around him. Our culture highly rewards such people with success, money, and power. On the other hand, their style of life is hard on them physically and emotionally and tends to cut them off from others.

One effect of this kind of excessive output of Control energy is that the person will consume and exhaust herself at a rapid rate. People like this have been classified as "Type A" personalities, which are prone to physical breakdown, illness, and an early death.[13] These people literally expend their stores of physical energy before their life cycles are completed.

However, the excessive exercise of this type of power is

particularly harmful to others as well. The earth, especially, is a victim of Control behavior by the people upon her who apply their tendencies to Control to every aspect of the biomass: building and reshaping cities, constructing parking lots and highways, damming up rivers, clear-cutting forests, strip-mining the countryside, pumping underground water deposits to exhaustion, extracting oil from the earth's insides and spilling it upon her surface, or polluting her atmosphere and surface with the by-products of these acts.

Energy of this sort is felt as oppressive and is responded to with resentment. Passivity or aggression are common reactions to high-level expressions of Control; consequently, people who are controlling find themselves surrounded by people who are either angry, passive, or both. A majority of their social transactions involve dominating or being dominated, with the consequent power struggles and games.

When Control becomes a single-minded obsession, it can be very harmful. It should be emphasized, however, that used with conscience, Control is a worthwhile source of power which allows us to effectively deal with our environment. Control as a source of power, when it is not out of control, helps us to bring about desired results and prevent unwanted outcomes.

We are under many different kinds of pressures. Externally, people want things from us. There are the pressures of making a living, obtaining recreation, dealing with traffic, bureaucracy, muggers, mashers, heat, cold, damp, and rain. Internally, our feelings demand constant expression. Our capacity to control all of these forces is an important form of power. Control, per se, is not good or bad; it is Control gone-out-of-control that we need to guard against.

The Technology of Control

The control of other human beings and animals has

been developed into a technology called "behavior modification." This use of our powers of Control to achieve desired behavior operates by forcing behavior into two categories. "Good," "correct," "appropriate," or "moral" acts are rewarded and/or "bad," "incorrect," "inappropriate," or "immoral" acts are punished. If people can be confined in a jail or other institution (school, mental hospital) where the rewards and punishments can be strictly controlled, this can be used to effectively shape human behavior without their awareness. Equally effective are the sophisticated strategies used to control people who are not confined to an institution by people who are accustomed to dominating others. The rich and powerful have known how to manipulate their fellow human beings for a long time and have passed down their knowledge through the generations. The successful use of Control power is taught to their children by constant example and at prep schools and private universities. Books like *The Prince* by Machiavelli have been written for them, and they have lawyers, public relations experts, politicians, sociologists, psychologists, physicians, and other professionals at their disposal who have knowledge useful for controlling others. Their control skills are being constantly upgraded.

When developed to its most subtle and powerful extent, Control is not easily noticed; it takes place behind the scenes, quietly and effectively, preferably with a friendly smile in front. All of the major politicians and corporations that would like to run our lives have perfected effective methods of Control and are using them on use at every opportunity, through public-relations campaigns, advertising, and the media. Most people have difficulty believing that we are under the constant influence of controlling energies and will assume that those who feel those energies are "paranoid."

As I will explain later, paranoia is actually heightened awareness, and fear of Control is a valid emotion. We need only take a look at what happens when Control gets out of control to gain respect for those who are paranoid about it.

Control-Gone-Out-of-Control

Control can run amok in large and small ways. Most intimately, we can experience it when the control of our own feelings gets out of hand and we are no longer able to feel anything except hard, cold deadness. Mental and educational institutions, jails, and the military are fertile environments for rampant Control. At a national level, we see governments completely controlling the news, as in the Soviet Union. Or we see a section of the population totally subjugated, as in South Africa. Or we have oil companies dominating the entire energy field, as in the United States. Internationally, the World Bank controls every significant major economic transaction in the world and has the power of life and death over any minor government and uses it at will—as it did when it helped the CIA and the Chilean ruling class destroy Allende's democratically elected government.

The ultimate example of Control gone amok is Hitler's Third Reich, which in its drive to dominate the world became a complex mechanism of awesome proportions and effectiveness, in which German business and industry, the military, the media, the courts, and the German people all worked together to exterminate millions and millions of human beings, wipe out complete cities, subjugate whole countries, and almost succeed in its plan of total world domination.

We, in this country, are used to freedom and independence and don't seriously fear the Nazi type of Control-run-amok. So far we have been lucky; hopefully, our luck will continue, but we must not delude ourselves into believing that type of Control and domination can't happen here. We have a growing right wing in this country which, with powerful new political methods, using computers to locate supporters, and with sophisticated, psychologically effective propaganda and organizational techniques are winning elections, influencing, and intimidating our politicians by "targeting" and defeating prominent liberals in government.

"The New Right are not rabid crackpots or raving zealots. The movement they are building is not a lunatic fringe but the programmed product of right wing passion, plus corporate wealth, plus twentieth century technology—and its strength is increasing daily"; [1] their aim is complete control.

The New Right succeeded in 1980 in taking over the republican party and nominating Ronald Reagan. Reagan, a passionate right-winger, who promised the American people that he would return to us the days of wine and roses, was able to convince a large majority that he could accomplish that goal. It is an indication of how much the American people are invested in the Control mode that they overwhelmingly preferred Reagan's promise of the return of the seventy-mile-per-hour limit to Carter's programs for energy conservation. In general the Reagan-Carter confrontation was a choice between two images: hard boiled versus emotional, dominating versus meek, man on top versus man in the middle, Macho versus Feminist, Control versus an attempt to govern in a cooperative manner. The people overwhelmingly went for the Controlling image.

Unfortunately Reagan can do nothing to return to us the days of easy money, big cars and seventy-miles-an-hour speed limits, because the source of power of those bygone days was oil and unlimited natural resources, which neither Carter could nor Reagan can bring back. But the fact that people fell for that promise reveal their vulnerability to the notion that the Control mode can fix our ills.

The New Right capitalizes on this vulnerability. Even though the New Right uses life, children, freedom, and the family as its issues, it is in fact a Death movement. It favors the death sentence, corporal punishment for children, the submission of women (the defeat of the Equal Rights Amendment), uncontrolled ownership and sales of handguns, which kill about twenty thousand and injure 100,000 people every year, abolition of abortion rights (which would bring back black-market abortions and wholesale carnage of women), and the nuclear future (the poisoning and death of the biosphere). If it has its way the New Right will probably not massacre blacks, Jews or homosexuals; it will threaten life on a less obvious but equally massive scale. By pushing forward the nuclear energy program it will put energy under the exclusive control of the giant utilities and the oil companies. In order to avoid terrorism and nuclear accidents, the excuse for a police state will be provided which can be used to suppress dissent. By abolishing environmental safeguards and restrictions in order to aid the giant steel, oil, and auto industries to maintain control of our economy, it will bring us to the environmental disaster we are on the brink of now. By increasing the power of the military by huge allocations to the Pentagon's budget, which can only come out of social welfare programs, it will take power away from the general population and hand it to the leaders of the industrial-military complex. In short, the right wing's aim is to even further concentrate power into the hands of the few, who will then have vastly increased control over our destinies.

The New Right plans to make these changes by "targeting" and defeating liberal legislators, taking control of the national and state legislatures, and ultimately forcing a constitutional convention in which our Bill of Rights will be revised, much to the detriment of our civil liberties.

The New Right's program, if it suceeds, will return Control to those who have traditionally held it and are slowly losing it as our democratic process matures; the super-rich and the super-powerful.

Those of us who want a fair distribution of power to continue in this country will have to struggle against Control at all levels; personal, local, state, and national. In this book I am attempting to explain what Control is and how it works on a day-to-day, personal basis so that we may prevent others from controlling us and so that we can have the choice of giving up Control as a means of being powerful in the realm of the Other Side of Power.

11

HOW TO AVOID BEING CONTROLLED

I have outlined the various power plays which people use to manipulate each other in their everyday lives. I've done so in the hope that by understanding the specific transactions involved in specific power-plays you will be able to defend yourself against unwanted manipulation. Further, if you are a user of power plays and have a conscience about manipulating others, you will be able to better understand your own behavior and make changes toward operating differently.

The awareness that people have about power use varies a great deal and can be handily divided into four levels:

I can see a power play coming from miles away. I learned how to use power plays early in life, and I've spent the last ten years studying them in an attempt to understand Control power. Consequently, I'm fairly reasonably aware and I can see people's power plays in high relief as they use them to get me or someone else to do something I don't want to do.

I also am more aware of my own use of power plays, though it is easier to see them in others than to see and admit them in myself.

Other people, while not being so clearly conscious of what a power play is and how it works, are nevertheless aware of it when they are being manipulated and react with a reflex stiffening, a digging in of the heels, a silent resistance which can be very effective in fending off the power play.

Yet others are not immediately aware of being power-played and become conscious of being had, hours or days later, while brushing their teeth, or in the middle of the night. Very often that kind of delay in awareness results in an angry reaction which is squelched because it seems unreasonable. After all, we reason, we went along with the power play, so we can blame only our own stupidity. Too late now to change things. Nevertheless, we develop a resentful backlog that becomes part of an attitude toward the person who power-played us.

Finally, some people simply go along with what is wanted of them, never becoming conscious that they are being manipulated, though the cumulative effect of repeatedly submitting to people's power plays eventually cause them to feel bad without having any idea of why.

In addition to these four levels of awareness about being controlled by others, there are four levels of awareness about controlling others.

Some people, whom I will call "conscious manipulators," are completely aware of using power plays; just as conscious as the person who flicks a switch in order to turn on a light. To certain psychotherapists, salesmen, doctors, politicians, political organizers, and bosses, the manipulation of human beings is second nature; a straightforward process applied to further their aims with only their own conscience as their guide. When conscious manipulators meet resistance, their response is deliberate and systematic: they either escalate or withdraw to a safe position to wait for a better opportunity which they eventually use to advantage. They are not passionate and do not get angry or particularly involved. They operate to remain unnoticed; softly and good-naturedly. They are cold-blooded and they are in a powerful minority because they are effective.

A second group of people are instinctive power players.

They grow up in an environment in which power plays are used frequently and freely, and they learn to use them accordingly. Their use of power plays is semiconscious, not necessarily deliberate. They are hotheaded power players, who, when met with resistance, often lose control and escalate and tend to wind up getting less of what they want rather than more. Anyone who remembers Jackie Gleason in "The Honeymooners" knows what a hotheaded power player is like. When they raise children, they teach them how to power-play and then proceed to practice their skill with them. More often than not, the children of hotheaded parents can't wait to get away from them. But when they eventually do, they can't help continuing the hothead pattern with their spouses, friends, or their own children.

The third category of people are basically innocent. Due to their upbringing, they do not have power-playing skills and do not seem particularly aware that power plays even exist. They try to get things by innocently asking for them, expect to get them, and often do. They are surprised when they discover the extent to which some people power-play to control others.

The fourth type rejects the use of power plays due to a conscious decision based on a belief that it is better to cooperate than to compete and power-play to achieve what they want. They know power plays exist, know how to use them, and how to stop them, and know how to respond cooperatively. They, too, are a powerful, effective minority and often are defectors from the ranks of conscious power players.

These four types of power players—the cold-blooded, the hothead, the innocent, and the cooperative person—often meet and interact. This is what happens:

Hothead Meets Hothead (Uproar). The relationship between two hothead power players is usually one of escalation, or uproar. Two such power players will almost immediately come into an intense confrontation. They will either like or dislike each other strongly. If they happen to fall in love, they will abandon their power plays for the time being, but eventually their relationship will be one of constant, competitive hassling. They may start out hassling and never get past that stage. When hothead meets hothead, they usually have a good time for a while, but everyone else tries to get as far away as possible. Eventually, however, their relationship can become rather grim.

Hothead Meets Innocent (Subjugation). Typically, this is the relationship between men and women, since men are most intensely trained in the use of power plays, while women are trained to be accepting and eager to go along with what men want. In this situation, the hothead systematically gets what he wants from the relationship, with the innocent going along until eventually, years later, reality dawns and dissatisfaction and anger eventually overwhelm the innocent. At that point, the hothead cannot understand why the hereto compliant and satisfied partner is suddenly becoming bitchy and unwilling to go along. He may escalate his power plays, eventually using violence or threats of violence, and subdue the innocent, who now is no longer innocent, but mad as hell.

Innocent Meets Innocent (Harmony). When two people who are both innocent in power plays meet, the experience is one of harmony and easy communication. There is a flow of friendly feelings and mutual understanding. The meeting of innocent with innocent tends to go unnoticed in the world of Control power because innocents tend to have none and are therefore disregarded. But these connections often exist between women or members of the Third World or other oppressed subcultures. The relationship between the meek, gentle people of this world need to be noticed and understood, because, as the Bible says, it is they who shall inherit the earth. From them we can learn how to be free of power plays with each other.

Conscious Manipulator Meets Cooperator (Struggle).

There are a number of other possible combinations between conscious, cold-blooded players, hotheads, innocents, and cooperators which I will not go into, but the confrontation between the conscious player and the cooperator is one of particular importance. I am interested in this relationship from the vantage point of the cooperator, which I am endeavoring to be myself. The cold-blooded power player is used to living in a world in which things happen according to his desires. He is convinced that what he wants is reasonable, and he believes that to use manipulative methods, including force, to achieve those goals is legitimate, and proceeds to do so. He will take the offensive to get what he wants. How hard he power-plays depends only on how much energy he has at his disposal.

If she is hired to be a manipulator, she will spend forty hours a week at it. If she is being a manipulator on her own, she will spend all of her waking (and maybe dreaming) hours at it. Very often she operates in a team with others who share her views; and if her team is large enough, she may be in control of enormous amounts of wealth and power. Whether she operates by herself or in a team, she is liable to be powerful because most people in the population are defenseless against an adept manipulator.

The cooperator, on the other hand, is interested in achieving things by having a maximum number of people participate voluntarily and without being manipulated. Consequently, the manipulator and the cooperator are at cross-purposes in almost any situation and their struggle is one that deserves to be documented. I will write about that struggle from the point of view of the cooperator, a person who understands power plays and is unwilling to go along with them or use them. The struggle between the conscious manipulator and the cooperator is illustrative of the issues which I am trying to raise here. The task of the cooperator in a struggle with a conscious manipulator is to identify and detect power plays and to influence the manipulator, without the use of power plays, into desisting from controlling others and becoming more democratic and cooperative in his behavior. Let us look at these steps in closer detail:

Identify the Power Play

Being skilled and knowledgeable in the area of Control and power plays is similar to being skilled and knowledgeable in any other area. A person who is skilled will sense a manipulator's purpose and will get warnings that a power play is being mounted. The power move is recognized and is responded to appropriately, and without panic. Being skilled and knowing power plays intimately is not to say that one does not get into tight spots or even succumb to them, but there is a sense of awareness of what is happening and of what to do about it in order to best avoid difficulty.

Deflect the Maneuver

The strongest tendencies when one is power-played is to retaliate with a stronger power play (escalation) or to give in (submission). The cooperative response is poised between these two extremes. Before anything is done the impact of the power play has to be deflected. Most often, when the power play is subtle, it is sufficient, simply, not to respond. For instance if the power play is "Yougottobekidding," it is enough, in order to deflect the power maneuver to say nothing. That doesn't solve the problem, but it stops the power play, since to be effective the maneuver requires a response from the victim. On the other hand if the power play involves fast talk or interruption, it isn't enough to be silent, since that will be seen as acquiescence and be taken as a license to continue in that vein.

The latter example is a good opportunity to use the Universal Power Play Stopper. This handy little gadget works amazingly well in almost any situation where a power play needs to be deflected. It is lightweight, handy, and can be carried in the hip pocket for instantaneous use. The name of this little marvel is WAM (or Wait a Minute!). WAM is effective in most situations as a power-play stopper; but if the power play has more than ordinary energy, WAFM (Wait a Fucking Minute!) will probably do the job. WAM disrupts the flow of a power play—it is a Control stopper, a sentence that can be used under almost any circumstances in which you are feeling that something is not right, or that you are about to do something you don't want to do or that the wool is being pulled over your eyes. It gives you a chance to stop, think, take another look, and decide what you want to do about a given situation. WAM can be said gently, as in "Excuse me, I would like to wait a minute before I make up my mind," or forcefully—"Now, wait a fucking minute!"—depending on the energy of the manipulation being tried. It needs to be used forcefully enough to have the power parity to stop the power play, but not so forcefully as to be an escalation. Accordingly it will not do to sweetly say, "Excuse me, I would like to think this over" to someone who has his or her hands around your throat. Nor will it be correct to roar, "Wait a fucking minute!" to someone who interrupts you in mid-sentence. Fortunately, WAM and WAFM have a flexible range adaptable to almost any circumstance.

Choose a Creative Strategy

Having deflected the power play and stopped the flow of controlling energy, there is now time and space to think the situation over. If nothing is clarified by a second's reflection, we can ask for a minute or we can ask for an afternoon, or overnight before we act. "Those are interesting statistics you are giving me, Mr. Smith. I would like us to spend some time checking them at the library."

Or "That is a difficult choice you are presenting me with,

Ms. Anderson, I have to discuss it with some of my friends."

Or "I'm not sure that I understand what you are proposing to me and I would like to ask you some questions to reassure myself that I understand you."

Or, "I believe that you are attempting to intimidate me, Jack, but I'm not afraid of you and it is clear to me that I do not want to do what you are suggesting."

This is a good time to talk with other people, read a few books, sleep on it, consult with your dreams—in short, bring into play information about the situation. There is no point in acting hastily; sometimes only a period of time will bring the needed creative alternative to people's consciousness. Getting information to make a good decision can take days; at other times, it may take just a few seconds to realize what we really want. When we take time to figure out the power play and to recall the antithesis and cooperative response to it, we gain the strength and the practice to exercise the disobedience and opposition to other people's manipulations which is necessary to replace Control with Cooperation.

Sometimes, in the ongoing struggle to fend off people's power plays, it is OK to let things slide. Maybe it's Friday night and you are tired, or you are otherwise occupied, or you are just not up to it right now. At such a time, you may choose to deal with the situation by using an antithesis and having done with it for the moment.

You may be surprised to hear me say this: sometimes it seems that you are the only person who wants to stop power plays, give up Control, and live in a cooperative manner. To let things slide seems a major setback. But that is not so. The desire to work together, to share, to take care of each other, and to cooperate is profound in people—in fact, in all species of animals—as Kropotkin shows in his book, *Mutual Aid.* Like a seed buried deep in our hearts, cooperation waits for the conditions in which it can flourish. Our job is to prepare the ground as best we can by learning about Control and power plays and by behaving as decently as we know how and as our endurance allows.

There are hundreds of thousands of people in this country alone who believe in the cooperative struggle. Cooperative nurseries and child-care centers, health clinics and food stores, agricultural cooperatives, democratically owned workplaces and land trusts, alternative birth centers, newspapers, filmmakers; the list is endless. You can get an idea of who is involved in the *Guide to Cooperative Alternatives.*

The people involved in these various projects all agree on one thing: they want to work together as equals, without power plays. They want to put an end to power abuse and hierarchies, they want to live without violence, and without nuclear power. And they want it bad enough to be willing to work at it long and hard. So when you find yourself tired and discouraged with a particularly difficult conscious manipulator, take heart: you are not alone, we are all in this together and we all have our cooperative nature on our side.

PART THREE:

Giving Up Control

12

LETTING GO

So far I have given you an idea of how Control works and what you can do to prevent people from controlling you. That is all well and good. Perhaps you have found it a little more difficult to accept that it is worthwhile not to respond to power plays with power plays. We are so steeped in the pleasures of Control that it is hard to give up the joy of sandbagging and flattening somebody who, obviously illegitimately and with malice aforethought, is trying to push us around. This book probably would do very well if it was called *How to Stop People from Pushing You Around and Make Them Wish They Were Sorry for Trying,* but that is not my aim.

However, let us assume that you accepted the dignity of a self-defensive rather than a retaliatory attitude about someone who power-played you. Yet, it might still be difficult to accept the validity, wisdom, or practicality of wanting to find a cooperative solution with him. I have been asking you to kiss your enemy rather than kill him.

But, as if that weren't enough, I am going to go further yet; I am going to suggest, now that we know how to prevent others from Controlling us, that we can and should give up trying to Control others altogether.

Assuming that you have agreed with most of what I have said so far, I am ready to press my case to convince you to take that leap of faith which is necessary to the letting go of Control in order to be able to make room for the Other Side of Power. Giving up Control and filling the power vacuum left behind as we do so is the topic of this section. In the following chapters, I intend to be very practical because I want to provide you with something which you can actually do and participate in—not just read about and forget.

You might comment that in asking people to give up Control, I'm biting off a mouthful. I am only planning to do away with centuries of tradition—a system which runs the "civilized" world—and replace it with some vaguely defined ideas which sound at the outset like a watery kettle of fish. After all, we are talking about rebelling against obedience, hierarchies, respect for authority; the leader-follower relationship. My response is that you are right: I am asking for a great deal, but I am promising a great deal, too. I am promising you power, which, like the other side of the moon, most of us cannot see and can only imagine. I am promising you the experience that comes with being a powerful individual living in harmony with yourself and with others as well as with your environment. I promise you the peace of mind and satisfaction that comes from the knowledge that to the best of your ability you are being a good and fair person. The way Control holds sway of our lives affects many facets of our behavior. The way we use our bodies, the way we converse, the way we make love, the way we treat people who have less power than we have, the way we feel about women if we are men, about children if we are grown-ups, about old people if we are young, about people of color if we are white, about poor people if we are economically comfortable, about gay people if we are heterosexual, the way we feel about single people if we are in well-functioning couples are all affected by Control power and are all in need of scrutiny and possible change.

Body Language

The first time that I became aware of the extreme subtlety and omnipresence of Control in my life was in 1969, when Hogie Wyckoff proposed that we go on a date in which we switched gender roles. She wanted me to get an understanding of how it feels to be at the receiving end of the subtle and not-so-subtle forms of control behavior which occur between men and women. She was to act as the "man" and I was to act as the "woman" for the whole evening. This experience was at first amusing, later alarming, and eventually mind-boggling.

We had agreed that she was to pick me up in her car. As I waited for her, I consciously exaggerated my concern for what I was wearing and how I looked. I peered in the mirror, looking for blemishes, and worried about whether she would be happy with my appearance.

She was to have picked me up at 6:00. At 6:05, she called me up.

"Sorry, but I was held up by an important phone call. I'm on my way right now."

That meant that she was going to be about fifteen minutes late. At 6:15 I heard her car in the driveway, and the honk of her horn. I was ready to go and since we were late, I thought I should possibly go out to the street. But being a little irritated by her presumption, I stayed put. A minute later she ran up the stairs, two steps at a time, and loudly banged on the door. I took my time to get to the door, opened it, and there she stood, full of energy, as if nothing at all was wrong.

"Hiya, cutie. How're ya doing?" she beamed.

I, happy to see her, smiled back, and answered, "Fine. Do you want to come in?"

"No, let's get going." I went back inside to get my coat, and as we rushed down the stairs, she asked, "Well, where do you want to go tonight?" Before I could answer, she continued, "I'll tell you what. I have a great idea. Let's go to Giovanni's."

I wasn't sure that I wanted to eat Italian food that night, but it did seem like a good idea, and since I had no other suggestions, I happily agreed. She walked me to the passenger side of the car, opened the door, and helped me in. I dimly appreciated the convenience of not having to open and close the door when getting into a low-slung car like hers. She strutted around the front of the car, looking gorgeous, and flashed me a smile. Opening her door, she got in, and before starting the car, she leaned over, and with one hand on my leg, and the other on the back of my neck, pulled me toward her, giving me a kiss smack in the middle of the mouth. As we drove to the restaurant, I noticed, for the first time since I'd known her, that she was a good driver, expertly passing cars, and accurately turning corners. I was also slightly uncomfortable at her speed, pressing my feet against the floorboard. I hesitated to put on my safety belt; I didn't want to offend her with what would seem to be a lack of confidence in her driving. While she drove, she spoke animatedly, sometimes looking away from the road in order to gaze at me, without interrupting the flow. We were in love with each other and happy to be together. My slight discomfort at being in the passenger seat (I usually drove when we went out) was a very minor feeling, compared with my excitement and elation at being with her.

As we walked to the restaurant, she held my arm above the elbow and, ever so slightly, guided me down the sidewalk. It was a crowded street, and she avoided collisions with other pedestrians by jogging slightly to the right and to the left, always indicating by a pressure on my arm, the direction she wanted to go. I complied. She opened the restaurant door, and as we got inside she stepped in front of me and signaled the maitre d'.

"A table for two, please, in the back of the restaurant. We would prefer a booth. Thank you." We both noticed the host's puzzled look and were amused by the situation. She was definitely feeling happy about it, and I was showing a good sense of humor as well.

We ordered drinks while we waited, and when the host came toward us, attempting to ignore her, he said to me, "Your table is ready sir." Hogie stepped between us and led the way. Slightly startled, the maitre d' led us to the table. I sat first, while she pushed the chair under me, and I thanked her.

Our role reversal was to be complete. As I looked at the menu, I thought to myself, "I can order anything I want . . ." But then, I reasoned, I shouldn't be greedy, and settled on a reasonably priced dinner. When she saw what I ordered, she said, "You don't want to eat that. Listen," she purred, "I recommend that you have the veal parmigiana. It's really good here." As she said that, she stroked my thigh under the table.

I was getting a bit confused. For one thing, she seemed to be enjoying this charade immensely, while I was getting slightly uncomfortable. I couldn't tell exactly why I was getting uneasy, but something was not right in the situation. It was acquiring the proportions of a task rather than being a game, and was beginning to interfere with my pleasure.

I said nothing, and the rest of the meal went on uneventfully; both of us had a good time. After dessert and coffee, she asked for the check, ostentatiously paid for the dinner, left a tip, and led the way out of the restaurant with me following closely behind and feeling sheepish.

Outside, we walked down the street.

"Let's do some window-shopping. There are some nice stores around here."

I agreed.

We went from window to window, as she stopped whenever she wanted to look at something. She moved on, stopped, and moved on and stopped, while I tagged along. At some point, I wanted to linger at a window, and after giving me an indication of her wish to go on, which I ignored, she actually pulled me with some force. I resisted and pulled back. She gave me a somewhat startled look, let go, and moved on to the next window.

Confused, I stood still for a few seconds and then rejoined her down the street. Clearly, the tension between us was mounting. We came to a corner. As I was about to cross, she stopped at a newspaper stand and looked at the headlines. I had one foot off the curb when I realized that she was not coming my way. In fact, having finished looking at the newspaper, she decided to cross the other street and was clearly indicating with her posture where she intended to go. I stepped back on the curb and joined her.

At this point, I was definitely irritated. I was silently considering whether I should bring up my irritation, but it became plain to me that there was nothing really to complain about. I needed simply to say, "I want to cross the street this way, instead of that way."

"Let's cross this way," I said, and she answered, "Well, all right. What difference does it make?"

"No difference. I just want to go this way."

"Sure. No problem." And from then on we went to the car with me in the lead.

As we sat in the car, there was an uncomfortable silence between us. I was feeling guilty for being irritated and making an issue out of such a simple matter. She was silent and withdrawn. After a while, she started on a new topic of conversation. The ice broke, and we talked animatedly. As she drove, she touched me with her right hand, stroked my hair, pulled on my moustache, caressed my thigh, and was clearly feeling tender and amorous. I was still concerned with my anxiety and irritation, and was not feeling very responsive. Nevertheless, I appreciated her gentle tenderness.

"Your place or mine?" she asked.

"Let's go to my place," I answered.

"Okay, but I was wondering . . . I've got a beautiful new record that I want you to hear. Let's go to my place. What do you think?" I agreed.

By now you are probably getting the idea of how this role reversal affected me. Not only was it startling to experience in how many ways the male role dominated my space and impaired my choices, but the complexity of emotions which accompanied the situation was amazing as well.

By the time we got to her place, I was in a definitely

black mood. She continued in our role reversal, undaunted. She became aggressive sexually; I became further confused. To make a long story short, for the first time in my relationship with her, I experienced a lack of sexual interest and when I tried to ignore this I was unable to my amazement and humiliation to muster the necessary erection.

I hope this elaborate example will accomplish the following: For people who are habitually in a passive position (this often happens to women), this example might explain some of the feelings that you experience when you spend time with someone who puts out strong, controlling body language. It might help explain the nagging, confusing irritation which grows very gradually out of a series of little, almost insignificant power plays. Each little acquiescence doesn't seem worth noticing; but as they add up, the net result is that you wind up feeling angry, frustrated, turned off, and drained of energy without really knowing why.

For the person who is habitually in control, this example can give you some idea of how your behavior affects others. You are not likely to really understand how it feels to be with you unless the shoe goes on the other foot; unless someone systematically succeeds in controlling you in a similar way. Voluntarily switching roles in this experimental manner will give you a very good beginning notion of what it is like to be in the company of a person who embodies control in every move toward you.

In this example, Hogie's controlling behavior was accomplished primarily through body language. When we switched roles, her physical behavior changed from the usual. She leaned in my direction, towered over me, touched me, held me, pushed me, pulled me, and invaded my space in a way that I had literally never experienced before in my adult life. Because her invasion of my space was loving—that is, it was primarily affectionate and nurturing—it was also confusing. I had experienced that kind of pushiness minus nurturing from dominating and aggressive males, who, without touching me, invaded my space with their voice, their gestures, and their energy. In those cases, however, my feeling was one of clear resentment and rejection, but with Hogie, her intrusion was supposedly loving; so why did I get so disturbed?

The answer to that question requires that we be able to separate different levels of energy from each other in our awareness.

Control is one form of energy. Love is another. I wanted to be loved by Hogie, but I did not want to be controlled. Her action mixed both types of energy, and my reaction was therefore mixed. There is a certain temporary pleasure in being controlled at times; when someone else is in charge we can forget our responsibilities.

Women are said to enjoy being controlled by strong men who believe women will behave accordingly when they try to please them. But even if a woman initially responds positively to male control, it is likely that in time she will lose her taste for the "Me Tarzan, You Jane" way of life. This may take years but it will happen; people don't like to be controlled for long even if they do at first.

The Invasion of Personal Space

Controlling body behavior doesn't necessarily involve physical contact. It is possible to control others through body language, at a distance. To understand this it is useful to realize that our bodies do not end at the surface of the skin. Our skin is the outside boundary of our body only in terms of what is visible to the human eye. But our body extends beyond our skin for at least a few inches, and some people will say for a much larger space than that. To illustrate this, let me suggest an experiment involving a couple of dime-store magnets, a nail, and a metal file. Set one of the magnets on the table. To the naked eye, it does not extend beyond the dark metallic bar which you can see. Let's call what you see the visible body of the magnet. However, everyone has learned in school that a magnet has an invisible (but very real) magnetic field. This magnetic field can be made visible by taking some iron filings (made by rubbing the file over the nail). Put a piece of paper on the magnet and sprinkle the filings over the magnet. You will see the filings arranging themselves in a pattern. Now that this demonstration has made the magnetic field of the magnet visible for you, remove the paper and look at the magnet again. In addition to the metal bar that you see, there is a very real, though invisible, field of force that surrounds it. You may actually be able to visualize that field and "see" it whenever you see a magnet in the future. You will then be seeing the magnetic body of the magnet. The visible body pertains to one level of energy: light waves. The magnetic body pertains to another level: electromagnetic waves. Both are real and both affect what happens to the magnet.

Hold one magnet between the thumb and forefinger of one hand and take the other between the thumb and forefinger of the other hand. Now visualize the fields of the two magnets as you move them slowly toward each other. If you pay attention to the forces in your fingers, you will experience how the two magnets interact with each other. You may feel a point, as they approach, when there's a force pulling them to each other, or you may feel a force repelling them from each other, depending on how you're holding them.

I use this example to illustrate something that happens between people in quite a similar way. Each person has a field of energy that surrounds her visible body, and extends beyond it, all around it. When another person approaches you, her energy impinges on yours. If you're tuned in to that level of energy, you can actually experience her energy field. At three feet away, the experience will probably be quite faint. Two feet away, you might begin to feel a definite presence. One foot away, the presence will be unmistakable. And as the person gets closer, your experience can become extraordinarily intense—especially if she strongly repels or attracts you, to begin with.

In our intimate human relationships, we spend a lot of time in each other's space, within that three-foot limit. How we use our energy with each other in that space is a very important fact of our everyday life.

Have you ever had the experience of someone speaking to you and standing uncomfortably close? This sometimes happens with someone from another culture, where conventions about space differ from ours. But some people are simply accustomed to crowding others physically. If it made you uncomfortable, that person was probably trespassing on your personal space. Have you ever gone camping and, looking for privacy, found an area on which to lie down that was just comfortably far enough from somebody else's campsite? And then has a third party come to lie down between that other person and you, causing you to feel invaded? Here again is an example of how we stake out a certain area beyond our body which we would like to keep private and free of intrusion.

The subtleties of personal space have to do with the aura of energy that we carry with us, and body language is a way in which people relate to each other, through that unseen but very real energy field which surrounds each of us. Most of us want certain distance from most other people. If we become attracted to someone, we open our personal space up and include that other person in it. If someone we are not ready to accept in our space intrudes or pushes on it, we feel extremely uncomfortable. Unfortunately, it is the experience of most women that many men take liberties with their personal space. And that is one of the fundamental aspects of sexism to be dealt with later in this chapter.

If you are a man who is trying to learn to give up control in relation to women, or a grown-up who is trying to treat children as equals, this discussion will have given you an awareness of the way in which your body language is a manifestation of your physical, though invisible, energy field, and how this energy field can be intrusive upon other people. If you are a Controlling type of person you need to take responsibility for all of your physical energy as it extends several feet outside of you, and then recognize the effect that it has on others. You might discover as you do this that you have been, effectively, a bull in a china shop, pushing around, disrupting other people's spaces, knocking things over, and in general, creating a wake of disturbance as you go through life, while being completely unaware of it. You can read a great deal more about this topic in Nancy Henley's book, *Body Politics*.

Here are some other things to be aware of: if you're large, your very physical presence may be intimidating to others. You need to carefully evaluate how close you can get to people, how fast you can move, and what your physical behavior needs to be in order not to be intrusive. If you are an average-sized person but you tend to move quickly, you will have a similar problem—not so much with the size and extension away from your energy field, but with its intensity. Your voice is an important aspect of your physical energy aura and projects beyond you. Is your voice loud and powerful? If so you should be aware of what it does to people, when you can use it fully, and when you need to subdue it. Men especially are capable of terrifying children and women with their voices.

If you are fond of touching others, you need to be especially careful because touch is definitely an intrusion into someone else's space. Most people enjoy being touched—but what kind of touch, how often, and where, are important questions to ask yourself in order to avoid being intrusive. If you're interested in further subtleties, you can analyze the kinds of clothing you wear, in terms of how it affects others with its color. Intense colors like white, yellow, and red will affect people differently from blue, green, and brown.

For people who are habitually Controlled this information can be used as a hint on how they can take some power with their touch, voices, clothing, and movements to expand their area of influence in the world in order to take a fairer share of their space.

Conversational Behavior

Another major way in which people control others is through their conversational behavior. Presumably, the actual purpose of any conversation is an exchange of points of view. We can disagree, work toward an agreement, or agree. But very often conversations do not have that aim at all, and are in fact attempts to control others through our words.

Under those circumstances, the situation is one where, if I have a point of view, and see that yours differs, I will do everything I can to change your point of view to mine, with you presumably doing the same, so that our conversation goes from being an exchange of ideas to being a battleground for thought control. Again, it is unfortunate that many conversations between people are often a struggle for control, rather than a cooperative exchange of ideas.

Interruption is the basic power play in a conversation. We interrupt when (a) we think we know what the other person is going to say, or (b) we don't like what the other person is saying, or (c) can't wait to make our point. People who interrupt others often feel that they are expediting and simplifying the conversation. On the other hand, people who are in the habit of being interrupted feel quite different about it. Here's a vivid account, by a friend of mine, on the effect of an interruption.

"Sometimes when I am interrupted in the middle of a sentence, I feel like a bird shot out of the sky. I literally feel like I hit the ground with a dull thud, head first, and I see sparks flying in my brain. My feelings are a combination of rage and hopelessness. I feel like I want to cry, and that I want to grab the interrupter by the neck and choke him until he is quiet. I feel like giving up. I feel like crying. I feel drained of energy. The task of regaining my train of thought and going back to what I was trying to say seems utterly hopeless. By that time, I have usually forgotten what I was talking about, and couldn't care less."

The opposite of interruption is listening, of course. Listening is a fine and difficult art. True listening involves attempting to understand how the other person is experiencing the situation. Not necessarily to agree with it, but to become fully aware of how that other person sees whatever it is that she is talking about. It is then possible to respond in a way which is not an attempt to control the other person, but to add our point of view to the conversation.

Very often women experience things differently from men. The same differences in how people experience things happen between grown-ups and children, white and black, poor and rich, and it is a natural outcome of the extraordinarily disparate ways in which these different groups of people have experienced the world. Often men's reactions to women's experiences (or grown-ups' to children's or whites' to people of color's or of young people's to old people's) are that they are incomplete, onesided (emotional), irrelevant, and/or irreverent. Or, their views are considered "cute," exciting, or childlike. Views that don't fit into the mainstream of ideas are rarely seen as valid and worthy of being adopted by "sensible" people.

When a person is having a conversation and disagrees, the first assumption should be that there is something about what is being said that isn't being understood. For instance, when Mr. and Ms. Smith discuss the best vacation spot, Mr. Smith fails to hear why Ms. Smith thinks that the mountains are healthier, cheaper, and more fun. He doesn't stop to try to understand why she sees it that way. He simply disagrees and tries to push his views on her. He should start out by assuming that her view has merit and needs to be taken seriously. If nothing that a woman (if you are a man) or a child (if you are a grown-up) or a person of color (if you are white) is saying has any merit in your eyes, you can assume that you are forcing your perspective onto her and taking for granted (on a purely sexist or agist or racist basis) that you are correct when she is not.

In order to listen, it is obviously necessary not to speak. Some people often believe that they are somehow responsible for carrying the conversational thread in a relationship. They feel that if they do not speak, nothing will be said. Consequently, they dutifully fill the space with their utterances. In fact, most women have assumed that men will direct, if not carry, the conversation in the same way in which they assume (as we will later see) that men will carry the sexual relationship as well.

One way in which it is possible to dominate someone else in a conversation is to overagree. Here the listener shakes his head up and down and makes various noises of agreement all with the purpose of saying in effect, "What you are saying is absolutely true—in fact it's perfectly obvious—and I knew it all the time, so you can skip it. Now here is how *I* feel about it."

When I am in a conversation, I perceive the space between the participants as a large container filled with contributions from the different people in the conversation. Sometimes everyone pours in large quantities of energy, and the space is full. In fact, sometimes it overflows with conversational energy. Other times, very little is put in, resulting in a barren and empty sensation. I try to contribute from my own reservoir into the space between myself and others in an amount which corresponds to my fair share. I don't like to put in too much, or too little. If the others don't contribute, I tend to feel uncomfortable because there is a pull on me to contribute more, which I don't want to do. Sometimes I just like to listen, but often, if the other people talk too much, I also feel uncomfortable because I don't like being crowded out. I'm usually happiest when everyone contributes equally.

Because of my upbringing I have a tendency to be a controlling person; I have experienced situations where I unwittingly became the focus of a conversation, with everyone looking at me and literally sucking me in with their attention. I was no longer at the edge of the circle, participating equally, but in the center. For a long time, I assumed that at those times I was being enjoyed by others.

Otherwise, why the rapt attention? Personally, I felt uncomfortable by the one-sidedness of the dialogue, yet flattered at the same time. In any case, I felt that I could not stop talking even if I wanted to. Every time I tried to stop, someone asked me a question or threw me a straight line—and I was off and running again.

Not until I began to insist on equality in conversation did I understand other people's experience of me in that kind of situation. One time I found myself quietly listening to another fellow who had gotten caught in the focus of a conversation. Harry seemed pompous, self-satisfied, and, frankly, obnoxious. The more he talked, the more uncomfortable and annoyed I got. I listened to him in fascination, silent and unhappy. Suddenly I realized that this was a familiar event. He was practically being forced into a controlling mode by our passivity. He needed help. At an opportune moment, I broke the spell by intruding with a comment on a new topic. Then, by asking a question of another person, I was able to withdraw from the center of attention which was now temporarily focused on me.

Operating in this way is a good example of how, if you give up your Control behavior, you are likely to discover opportunities to exercise other forms of power. Because I have given up Control in conversations, I have been in a position to experience a whole set of new possibilities. I have had the opportunity to listen, empathize, learn non-controlling communication, and to help boring, one-sided conversations become more interesting by involving everyone—not just a few verbally skillful people.

Sexism

Sexism is the system of domination of women by men. It is deeply rooted in both men and women, who after systematic indocrination by schools, media, and parents, accept that men's role is to control and dominate women. Giving up sexism is a "subagenda" for men and women of the larger program of giving up the Control mode in general.

True, it isn't *always* the case that control is wielded by men. Women are sometimes in the place of power as owners of businesses, inheritors of their dead husband's or father's power, and as overbearing wives and mothers. Some women have great power; but, let's be honest about it, they are still the exception rather than the rule. When women have Control power, it has usually been ceded, inherited from, or allowed by men. The fact is that the lion's share of the power to control, dominate, manipulate, destroy, give, and take away is in the hands of men, not in the hands of women.

The Control experience is typically the male experience, even though some women have recently been allowed to share in it. Patriarchy is the rule, men make the decisions, have the power, and hang onto the privilege.

In the lowest rungs of power, where both men and women have practically none, the hold of men over women seems to relax a bit and that is because he absents himself—loses interest, becomes disabled, goes to jail, or dies. Among the poor, very old, and Third World people, women have a stronger role and place than among the white middle-aged, middle-class, and rich. But even where a woman's role is stronger and allows her considerable control over significant issues, such as child-raising and economic matters, the man has the ability to use his greater physical strength to establish his ultimate mastery. Nowhere is the fact of male supremacy more evident than among poor peasants and working people, where both men and women alike have to struggle daily to survive. And when the day's work is done, the woman waits on the man and takes care of the children. She works a full day alongside the man and another day serving her family.

Michael Korda, who, in my estimation, understands a great deal about the subject of patriarchy, makes it plain that men have all but a tiny portion of the power in this world and that "every effort will be made to prevent [women] from having real [Control] power." Anyone who questions this assertion should read his chapter on women in his book *Power,* in which, so far as the business world is concerned, he proves the point overwhelmingly.

Power plays—Competion—Control—Patriarchy: all four are intimately tied together. It is because of this that, when I speak of giving up Control, male chauvinism becomes an important practical example with which to work. Male chauvinism—or sexism—is based on the control of women by men. The way men overpower women—and women's reactions to this—is central to many people's lives and a source of the day-to-day difficulties between the sexes. The process of giving up sexism takes time, patience, a dogged commitment on the part of the man, and loving patience on the part of the woman (or women) he relates to. It is important here to realize that women often perceive their relationship with a man who wants to become a practicing feminist as a mixture of enjoyment and hard work. A man who knows a woman who is willing to walk alongside him while he stumbles and falls in his struggle to give up Control (after repeatedly knocking her down in the process) is indeed lucky. Such a woman is a gift from the Goddess and should be appreciated and thanked, generously and often. Likewise, a man who is willing to give up his control and to share with women his powerful skills is also to be appreciated. It is not easy fighting sexism, for women or men. All those who do deserve praise and recognition.

For women, giving up sexism implies taking power, refusing to go along with the comforts of being taken care of by men, and relinquishing the fantasy of being under a strong man's wing. It means planning to learn a number of skills which have become men's domain and to "go it alone" whether in opening reluctant jars, learning about cars, or becoming physically strong and agile. It means giving up the obedient-cute-mother-housewife image in favor of a self-sufficient, independent, powerful self-image. This can be scary since the world is inhospitable to independent women—especially if they are feminist, aggressive, powerful, and not exactly thrilled with men.

Giving up sexism for women has a clear goal: get out from under, be strong. Men's goals aren't as clear or attractive. Why should any man willingly abandon the privilege of being a man? Why should he give up his advantage as a wage earner, his superior strength, his rights in marriage (to be looked after, laundered and cooked for), his privilege to have the first and last word? In short, why should he give up the upper hand in the power to control his relationships? What's in it for men? Let me give you some reasons, starting with the most attractive though not necessarily the most important.

Would you (I am speaking to men now) like to live longer, work less hard, feel less burdensome responsibilities in your life? Giving up Control will help you to love and nurture yourself. It will make you more aware of your health and teach you how to ask for and accept help to share your burdens.

Would you like to be able to love more fully and reliably? Giving up Control will help you contact your feelings and teach you how to be a loving person. Would you like to be able to think more creatively, solve problems more effectively? Giving up Control will teach you less rigid (black-or-white, all-or-nothing) ways of thinking. It will help bring the creative solutions to your mind.

Would you like to have better friendships (with men as well as women) and work relationships? Would you like to have more fun? Again, giving up Control will help.

Would you like to contribute to a world in which men no longer make all the basic decisions and in which women are able to influence events and have power? Your individual decision to give up Control over women—to embrace feminism—will help bring about that goal. In order for the ruling-class men to give up control of world resources and money, government, science, healing, and spirituality, it is necessary that we, who are their unwitting followers and servants, reject that system of Control which dominates our lives. And in our individual lives that system is reflected in sexism, and patriarchal hierarchies, not just as practiced by men upon women but as practiced, it seems, by all of us, men *and* women, who have any power over the less powerful.

THE WOMEN'S MOVEMENT

The women's liberation movement has gone through a number of phases since it reawakened in the 1960s.

At first it was an extremist radical movement led by women half-crazed with righteous anger about the intolerable oppression they experienced. The bra-burners and the women of SCUM (Society to Cut Up Men) hit the headlines and drew the public's attention. The media quickly trivialized the women's movement by focusing on the radical aspect of it.

Anger was then a distinguishing feature of the movement. Women developed consciousness-raising groups where men were not allowed. As a higher awareness of sexism developed, it became increasingly obvious to more and more women just how men exercised their control over them. Within the women's movement, the lesbian women's movement developed its own power. Women weren't just having meetings without men; other women were becoming woman-identified women who resolved to do without men altogether.

The anger and energy which the women's movement generated was effective in bringing about major changes in people's awareness.

Years of struggle followed in which women made some gains in salaries, access to power, reduction of sexist language, and abortion rights. A few men joined as sympathetic, helpful followers who lent their power to the movement wherever needed. Feminism was no longer just the serious concern of women, but of men as well. Some women who were committed feminists began to see some men as allies in a common struggle.

In the last few years, the "women's lib" fad has passed. There have been significant gains, but the antifeminist backlash is upon us. It is once again common practice to refer to women as girls, the ERA may be defeated, many women openly disassociate themselves from feminism though they unwittingly enjoy its benefits, and men continue to earn much more money than women. The salary gap is actually widening.

The work of feminism continues, but it is taking a very different shape from its original beginnings. It is less angry, often includes men, and goes under a host of different titles such as child care, rape counseling, cooperative living, affirmative action, skills and job sharing, self-help clinics, feminist gay liberation and feminist men's liberation, new laws and mores which allow women more and better choices in their relationships. Feminism has had a decisive role in the ecological movement, the antiwar and antinuclear movements, the nutrition and food revolution, and the holistic health movement.

MEN'S PROGRESS

As women become more powerful and men wish to relate to them as equals, men don't always make the transition from male chauvinist pigs to feminists very smoothly. Men aren't trained to be equals with women, and our tendency to be Controlling is deeply ingrained in us. So, as we try to give up active Control, we often simply switch into a more passive but still Controlling mode of behavior.

Control can be carried out in an active, outgoing way or in a passive or ingoing way. Energy can radiate out or be sucked in. When radiated out, it Controls by pushing against others. When going the other way, it Controls by pulling people in.

This passive Control approach is one that men have increasingly adopted as a response to the demands made upon them by the women's movement. Wanting to give up Control, they freeze in their tracks, and they withdraw from the fray. Now they sit on their energy. Most of the time, this is a sincere effort to control their out-of-control power behavior. While this is an inevitable first step in giving up Control for men, it certainly must not be the last.

Many men go through this process with strategic intent. The purpose here is not to give up Control but to Control their Control (a paradox not likely to work). This process is rather like sitting on a stiffly coiled spring and keeping it compressed through great effort. The obvious outcome is that ultimately we must let go, exhausted, and the coil will burst open to its full extension. In real life, a man who goes into this kind of strategic withdrawal of power behavior is like a time bomb. Women who relate to men in that phase are initially attracted by their apparent desire to be non-controlling but find that these men's Control needs gradually surface in subtle (or eventually, crude) power plays.

One obviously bitter woman provided this scenario: "There are a lot of guys hanging around these days who are real laid-back and 'groovy' even to the point of talking a good feminist line. But get close to them and somehow, sooner or later, they wind up on top; in Control, hanging on, and pushing hard. It's an uncanny, seemingly irresistible tendency not to be denied. I'll take a 'macho' man any day. At least you know what he wants and what you are dealing with."

This surfacing of Control behavior may happen even if the man is well meaning in his efforts to give up Control. The outcome is often as disappointing to the man as it is to the woman. To be a man in this situation is like being under the influence of an irresistible reflex. We watch ourselves respond automatically to situations that push our Control buttons and spoil situation after situation.

If you are in this phase of development, take heart! If

you stay with it, it will pass, and you'll be able to anticipate and eventually give up those automatically competitive reactions. It's part of the process of change. But don't stop at that point where you just look good enough to "pass" as a considerate, respectful, cooperative man. That alone is hardly an improvement over your old self.

Giving up Control doesn't mean giving up. It means establishing an exquisite balance of equality which requires everyone's involvement; those who are habitually one-down have to work just as hard as those who are habitually one-up, and constant, ongoing vigilance is needed to keep the will to Control or be Controlled at bay.

SEXUALITY

A very important area in which control manifests itself is in the sexual relationships between men and women. We know that big business, government, the military, the media, and all the major institutions of this country are dominated by men, but we fail to recognize how complete male domination is in sexual relations. Men dominate in every sphere of our lives, to an extent which is usually not obvious. Nowhere is this as hidden as in sexuality. But the illusion is that women are in Control.

This illusion is promoted by the fact that, by and large, men are much more eager to have sexual intercourse than women. As I understand it from conversations with many women, there are many reasons for women's reluctance. A major reason, still, is the fear of pregnancy. Men breezily tend to think that in these days of the Pill, the problem of birth control has been solved. But many women are no longer on the Pill, since their many serious side effects have become known. Those who are on it may have missed taking it and may be unsure that it is working at the time. Any other method of birth control carries a definite fear of pregnancy and anxiety level, no matter how conscientiously it is used.

Another reason is fear of genital infection, or irritation,

which is much more likely to occur with women than with men. With the recent epidemic spread of genital herpes, which is far more painful for women than for men, potentially lethal to newborns, and incurable, the specter of VD has once again become a powerful, valid reason for women to fear intercourse.

Many women are not eager to have sexual intercourse because they have experienced men's sexual ineptitude. Some men seem to be irresistible thrusters who feel that the ideal male needs to closely approximate a steam engine, banging deeply into them at high r.p.m. Other men climax within seconds of initiation of intercourse. These are only two of the major quirks that men suffer from when it comes to having intercourse. There are many others.

Some men will consider nothing but the man-on-top position (called the "squashed-bug position" by a friend of mine). Others are disgusted by female genitalia. Some become violent. Still others need to flee after intercourse, leaving mystified sadness in their wake.

In any case, women can do very little about these peculiarities, since most men's egos are very vulnerable to sexual criticism. Consequently, women tend to avoid getting into the position of having to deal with men's sexual idiosyncrasies. All of these reasons explain why a man who is known to be a considerate and sensitive lover is much more likely to encounter sexual acceptance by women.

These are not the only reasons why women avoid sexual intercourse. Women tend to take sexuality much more personally. To some men, having sexual intercourse is not much different from a warm, loving embrace. Women rarely feel this casually about sex. Often, a sexual experience tends to engage the woman emotionally more than it does the man. Women therefore often avoid sexuality for fear of getting involved with a man who is himself not involved; a very painful experience indeed. Of course, a woman may not want to have intercourse simply for moral reasons.

There are, probably, times when women may avoid having intercourse with men because this can be an effective way to control the man. A woman may feel that her control over the decision to have intercourse is the only power that she has and she may use her power in this way. It seems to some men that this is the main reason why women refuse sex. A man who holds to this point of view has few, if any, chances of endearing himself to a woman. He will ignore all the other reasons for her reluctance and deal with it as if it were a contest of wills. She will feel that she is in the hands of a subtle or crude rapist and, regardless of the many myths to the contrary, women do not like to be raped.

So yes, women do, by and large, control whether the exchange of sexual and emotional energy, which men so badly need, will actually take place, and they do at times use their power to withdraw their favors to manipulate men. Sometimes women will lead men into the tender trap and saddle them with responsibility and children by the device of withholding their sexuality. Men who feel that they are hunted by women as "meal tickets" are as justified as women who complain of being hunted as sex objects.

But every other aspect of sexuality is totally male-dominated. Women can control sex only by not having it. Once they decide to go along, they lose their position of power unless they withhold sex once again and that is not always effective since many men are only looking for one fast fuck—"Wham-Bam, thank you, ma'am," or for a quick ball game—"Three strikes and you're out."

ORGASM

It is a fact, when it comes to orgasm, that fewer women than men experience it. Men are occasionally unable to achieve orgasm, but this is rare in comparison with the lack of orgasm in women. The reasons are assumed to be rooted somehow within the woman. After all, we reason, men have no problems here; they can "come on a dime." Clearly, if the woman doesn't have orgasms, that must be her problem—not the man's.

Let's look at it another way. If you are a man, you probably learned, as I did, that the pursuit of sexual intercourse is an orderly business. It is part of a predictable series of events, one chained to another, beginning with making a date, ending in bed. In between these two, we learned to expect, roughly, the following sequence: Light touches on the arms and around the waist, followed by subtle caresses on the outside of the legs, neck, and hair; pursued by kisses on the ear, cheeks, and occasional strokes around the breasts; followed by kisses on the lips; going from dry to wet thrusting of the tongue, touching of the inside of the thigh, belly, and flank, massaging the breasts, nipples, and vagina, progressing to the bed, taking off clothing, inserting, thrusting, and orgasm.

When things "go well," the sequence is followed in a systematic way, with the man making the moves, the woman acquiescing and hopefully enjoying the progression. When the man finally decides to insert his penis and thrust, he is ready to come and the woman is expected to have an orgasm as well.

Often, this is not the case. When "it" doesn't come, the questions are "What happened? Why didn't she? What's wrong with her?" Yet it seems that, since women have become more aggressive and have taken sexual matters into their own hands, there has been a marked incidence of what is considered to be "male impotence." I can't prove that this is the connection, but I very strongly suspect that sexual control by women would lead to male sexual dysfunction of the same magnitude as that exhibited by women today.

To change this dismal sexual picture, it is necessary for women to become more sexually aggressive at the same time as men lie back and become less so.

But the tendency to Control is deeply ingrained in men. It is not surprising that we experience all sorts of difficulties when we want to be passive, yielding, or soft. For instance, men find it difficult to lie still and let a woman take the sexual initiative. As soon as we become sexually aroused, our irresistible tendency is to take over, climb on top, and thrust with abandon in pursuit of our almighty orgasm.

Women have the opposite tendency: to lie back and let the man do the work and take responsibility for her pleasure. The changes that need to happen are complex and need to be coordinated; if the woman becomes aggressive before the man is able to lie back, he will probably get angry or lose his erection. If he becomes passive while she remains passive herself, not much of anything is likely to happen except a good night's sleep.

BIRTH CONTROL

Men seem to expect women to take care of birth control. When sexual intercourse becomes a possibility, the man usually proceeds on his charted course and ignores the issue. If the woman is not prepared, she has to stop the man, tell him that she is not protected, and initiate a discussion of what can be done. (If she doesn't bring it up, the man assumes that everything is OK.) This is a grossly unfair approach. In many instances, when a man and a woman become sexually turned on to each other, the woman is not protected against pregnancy. She may feel embarrassment about discussing the matter, just as he would. She may feel reluctant about interrupting the sexual flow, or fearful he may be annoyed at her lack of foresight. She may not know to what extent he controls his ejaculation, and thus worry about his climaxing immediately after or before insertion.

In general, the whole subject is fraught with anxiety and confusion. To expect the woman to take the initiative in dealing with this problem is an extremely sexist attitude on both their parts.

A man who is serious about taking responsibility in this area will, as early as possible, when it seems they might have sex, bring up the topic and deal with it responsibly. If she is not on the Pill or does not happen to be wearing a diaphragm, a man should be willing to take responsibility of obtaining and wearing a condom. All birth control is a bother, and it is essential that men share the burden with women. Obviously, for the woman, the most convenient form of birth control is a condom. Unless she doesn't like the way it feels, it is the best from the point of view of safety and freedom from bother. The intrauterine device would seem a good method, too, but it has exceptional potential risks for the woman. Many women who wear them wind up having to take them out due to infections. Pregnancies occur in spite of them, they hurt when inserted, and occasionally one perforates the uterine wall. So again, like the Pill, it's convenient for the man, but dangerous for the woman.

Then there is the diaphragm. Inconvenient, not 100 percent safe, and some people don't like the way the spermicide cream feels or tastes.

So let me recommend condoms as a way for men to share the burden of birth control. First, if used properly, they are foolproof and safe. They don't require foul-tasting creams and when properly used (no artificial lubricants—the people's natural lubricants, spit, and/or tap water, applied generously inside the condom, work very well) they are quite satisfactory. Having to get up in the middle of love-making to put on a condom is a small step in equalizing the hassles of conception and contraception.

Finally, for men who have decided they don't want any more children, let me make a strong bid for vasectomy. Consider the enormous numbers of unwanted pregnancies and the monthly anxieties that sexually active women suffer, and compare it with the cavalier attitude many men have about matters of conception. It is highly commendable and appreciated when a man is willing to go through the discomfort and commitment that a vasectomy represents—especially when it is done to share the burden of birth control. A man who reads these lines and feels that he is being asked for more than seems fair should consider this. Any woman who has had one abortion has done more to share birth-control responsibilities than any man could do in a hundred years of wearing condoms; the anxieties related to the side effects of a vasectomy, realistic as they may be (though none have been proven to exist), are no different from the anxieties women have to cope with in relation to pregnancy, abortion, intrauterine devices, tubal ligations, and the Pill.

Another way in which a man can demonstrate his commitment to dealing with a woman on a noncontrolling basis is shown by his response to a woman's unwillingness to have intercourse if that is her choice. She may want to be loving, hug, kiss, cuddle, and even sleep with a man, and not want to have intercourse. If that is the case, a man should be willing to relate to her on her terms, rather than on his. He ought to be willing to explore satisfying alternatives to intercourse, such as oral sex, mutual masturbation, or even just masturbation while in her company (as a way of pleasuring himself while respecting her desires).

Most of what I have said in this section on sex has been thoroughly written about from the point of view of women in the book *Sex for Women,* by Carmen Kerr. I have only given a brief introduction to the issue of sexism in sexuality here. For a more complete review, I recommend her book.

LINGUISTIC OPPRESSION: ONE LAST POINT

You probably have noticed certain people who will invariably make a comment when someone refers to a woman as a "girl" at gatherings and at lectures, when someone continually uses the masculine pronoun to refer to both men and women, or whenever sexist linguistic assumptions are made in people's language. Very often that person seems to be a party-pooper, someone who obviously lacks a sense of humor and seems to want only to call attention to herself at the expense of someone else. To me, however, people who are willing to interrupt the flow of a conversation or gathering to make a valid point in relation to some form of power abuse are people who are particularly committed, and I support them fully.

To me, then, the badge of feminist courage is the willingness to object whenever the word "girl" is used to refer to a grown woman. To be sure, it's just a badge, and a badge does not a feminist make, but I believe it to be a meaningful activity.

Now you may respond to these paragraphs with irritation, thinking: "Why is he making such a big deal out of a word; it's only a word; I also call men 'boys' once in a while" or "I know many girls who dislike being called 'women'" or "This is ridiculous, but I'll go along with it because I'm not willing to hassle about it." These and other arguments that resist the very straightforward notion about the necessity to treat men and women equally, in our language at the very least, are very common reactions in men and even recently, in women. Let me explain.

Words have real power. It makes absolutely no sense to call a grown woman a "girl" while you call a grown man a "man," any more than it makes sense to call a black man a "boy" when you would not call a white man a "boy." Even if it is not your own intention to control women by calling them "girls," the fact is that the word, when used by men about women, has the effect of controlling their behavior. How? The word "girl" has associated with it less power, and implies sexiness, beauty, and youth, as opposed to maturity, intelligence, and strength. When you use "girl" in referring to a grown woman, you are wittingly or unwittingly contributing to a conspiracy to keep women in a lesser place. You are also being ageist; that is, you are subtly putting down older people. To see that, you have to be tuned in to the effect of language in people's lives; language is a powerful influence and in order to fully deal with Control, you will have to, in one way or another, come to validate the power of language.

It might be helpful, at this point, to share with you the definition of feminism that I accept. To me feminism is, above all, love of women.

It is out of love not moral outrage or missionary zeal that I make these points about language. Feminism has come to mean nastiness, anger, and hatred of men. True love for women can turn into outrage and zeal when abuse becomes intolerable, but love needs to remain the basic motivation. The main point is that if we love women we will treat them with respect and we will want others to treat them with respect and we will want to achieve this end lovingly.

Let me show you also that in the eyes of women, men have absolutely nothing to lose and everything to gain by making this distinction. True, there are some women who feel a bit uncomfortable when they are referred to as "women" and will admit that they prefer the word "girl" applied to them. If you ask, you will find that those women have accepted the notion that the word "girl" implies youth, beauty, sexiness, and attractiveness to men, while the word "woman" is more threatening because it is devoid of those particular implications. Further, "woman" implies maturity and power, which some women think turns men off. But in general, the word "woman" will make a woman feel good about herself and about you. It is a respectful word, a full-sounding word, and it shows you take her seriously. She will appreciate it.

The linguistic discrimination against women is so prevalent that it gives you an almost constant opportunity to practice your feminism. And the "girl" versus "woman" problem is, of course, only the beginning. You will find yourself in different situations where your principles will demand that you do something about a specific form of behavior which you have decided to struggle against, and this will give you an opportunity to learn the different techniques of effective, loving confrontation which are appropriate for the occasion.

Obviously, it will not do to deal in the same way with every situation in which a person calls a woman a "girl." The person may herself be a woman, or it may be basically a slip of the tongue as opposed to a conscious dig, or it may be an innocent usage. Or it may happen in the middle of an important statement which you do not wish to interrupt, or you may be exhausted and have no energy left for struggling on that particular day. Every one of these circum-stances would require a different approach or strategy, including, at times, doing nothing and waiting for a better opportunity. The aim of what you're doing is not to bring about changes through Control, since it is Control that you're giving up. As a consequence, you would not, for in-stance, judge, badger, or insult someone in an attempt to deal with his sexism. Nor do you want to put yourself in a place where you seem ridiculous. This will be an opportu-nity for you to practice powerful cooperative responses to a problem.

As an example, let's say that you're out with a group of friends. You're having dinner around the table, and one of the men in the group, speaking about an acquaintance of yours, says, "Oh, yes, I know Sally. She's a nice girl."

What are you to do? You could say, "Listen, Tom. I know you don't mean anything by it, but Sally is definitely a woman."

Or you could say, "Tom, I wonder how you stand on the issue of calling women 'girls?' Would you be willing to con-sider doing something about it? It makes me uncomfortable when you refer to Sally, who I know is a woman, as a 'girl.' "

Or, you could say, "Last time I saw Sally, she looked like a woman to me, and I know she's definitely over twenty-one."

Or, finally, you could suggest, "Well, if you really like Sally, I'm sure she'd appreciate your referring to her as a 'woman.' "

You can see that there are many ways of approaching this problem, and each situation has its own special require-ments. The main point is that if you are interested in giving up Control over women, as a man, then you will be aware of and willing to deal with every sexist situation, and you will attempt to do so with something other than Control power. You will go from the simple to the complicated, from the mundane to the sublime. But I believe that the "girl" versus "woman" question is a good place to start, especially now that the backlash against feminism is bringing the usage of "girl" back into the public ear.

Giving Up Control Over Children

The area in which giving up control seems most radical and risky and at the same time most desirable is with children. At the Round Mountain Cooperative Community where I live, our children are being brought into a world where, from the first moment, some of the most controlling experiences babies are usually subjected to are absent. They are being born on the ranch, among relatives and friends, without the unnecessary and oppressive features which have been added to childbirth by the health-care establishment. The births are symbolic of what the community stands for, namely a cooperative social context free of power plays. The baby is not taken from its mother in the first days and is fed whenever it wishes to eat. For the first months of the baby's life it is given whatever it seems to want whenever humanly possible.

As they grow older, because one of the guidelines of the community is that no power plays are permitted, children also are largely exempted from being manipulated into doing things that they would not otherwise do. No attempt is made to force a feeding or toilet-training schedule on them. While everyone is very conscious of power plays and whether they are used on children, there are a variety of points of view on the subject. Theoretically, commanding a child, physically removing it, spanking it, hitting it, or in any way punishing it is a form of a power play. Bruce Carroll, one of the ranch residents, for instance, has successfully raised a number of children to adulthood and holds the most radical point of view with respect to power plays with children: not everyone completely agrees with him but he believes that absolutely no power plays should ever be used with them.

Children *will* do what is right for them, given the freedom to choose and circumstances in which the choices can be made without stress or pressure. Power plays are not necessary to cause or help children to do what is good for them; they will do it on their own accord.

Take, for instance, the example of Mary, an eight-year-old who wants to stay up late on a weekday to watch television. Parents know that a child needs about ten hours of sleep to be able to function adequately, and most parents would be inclined to set a bedtime and insist that it be kept. Suppose now that Mary, who has to get up at 7:00 in the morning, wants to stay up beyond 9:00 in the evening. What are her parents' choices in this matter? Should they enforce a 9:00 bedtime by insisting on it and using power plays such as commanding, yelling, turning off the television, spanking, or maybe even forcibly undressing the child and putting her to bed if necessary? The parents in this situation are up against their own faith in human nature. If we assume that Mary is an intelligent human being capable of making valid decisions in the affairs that concern her, I would like her to exercise this capacity and trust her to choose well. As far as I'm concerned, Mary has the right to stay up as late as she wants, to get as little sleep as she will, and to be cranky all the next day if she so chooses.

You may ask, "What if she oversleeps and misses her bus and therefore has to be either driven to school or even to stay at home the next day?" Mary's selfishness of the night before might result in creating a large inconvenience for her parents the morning after.

Suppose that Mary stayed up late and overslept. Now she wants to stay up late once again. Her parents notice this and ask her to go to bed.

"Mary, I would like you to go to bed. It's past nine o'clock."

"But I want to watch this program, and it ends at eleven o'clock."

"I don't think that's a good idea, Mary, because last time

you stayed up, you overslept, and I had to drive you to school."

"I won't oversleep this time. I'll set the alarm."

Mother could now power-play Mary and force her to go to bed, or she could negotiate reasonable, cooperatively arrived at conditions.

"Okay, Mary, I still don't think it's a good idea. I believe you're going to have trouble getting up. But I think you should do what you think is best for you. However, I'm not going to try and get you out of bed tomorrow morning or drive you to school; and if you oversleep I would like you to walk to school, no matter how late. And if you are late for school again tomorrow, I am going to be very upset if you stay up late again on a school night. Okay?"

"Okay, Mom. Will you help me get ready if I am too sleepy?"

"Fine. Enjoy your program. I love you!"

Chances are that Mary will wake up and go to school in time. If she doesn't and has to walk to school, she will probably choose not to watch television next time rather than take a chance on being too sleepy in the morning. That's what most grown-ups do, so why not trust and give her the chance to learn just like we did? I have noticed that the main effect of this approach is that our children learn the same things we learned, in about half the time. It took me twenty-five years to develop the cleanliness and good study habits my children had by age twelve, and thirty years to learn the social skills they had by age eighteen. I look forward to having them around when they are thirty and sixty years old.

This example shows how it is possible to allow Mary to choose what she wants to do, to allow her to experience the consequences of her choice, without, at the same time, allowing her to interfere with other people's well-being. When Mary is given this kind of freedom in a host of situations, beginning as soon as she is able to make such choices, she will grow accustomed to making decisions which are based on her own judgment. Her judgment will eventually include her responsibilities toward others and their feelings. Children who are obedient and follow orders become accustomed to doing things as they are told without understanding why. Children raised under this kind of program are mysteriously expected, once they are emancipated, to suddenly be able to make decisions and choices on their own. The fact is that most children's upbringing gives them no opportunity to choose, gives them no opportunity to experience the consequences of their choices, and gives them no opportunity to make cooperative choices which respect the rights and feelings of others.

But suppose now that the reason why Mary stays up late at night has something to do with the fact that she really doesn't want to go to school and that she would rather watch television than ready herself for school the next morning. She may even secretly hope that if she stays up late she will oversleep and not have to go to school. What are parents to do—since at this point Mary would not only welcome missing the bus and perhaps even not being driven to school? This is a more complicated situation. What are parents to do about the fact that some children don't like to go to school and that they'll do anything to avoid it? Let me answer this question with another question. What interests you more: freedom, or school attendance? Do you want to bring up children to do things they don't enjoy and which are not likely to be good for them? If a child does not enjoy school, chances are that the school is not a good place for the child. Faith in our children demands that we assume that they will be interested in learning when learning is interesting, that children want to go to school when school is a good place for them. It stands to reason that if school is a nasty, uptight, competitive place filled with social and racial strife, authoritarianism, power plays, and injunctions against spontaneity, awareness, and intimacy, children might want to stay away from it. But the law says children have to go to school. So what are parents to do?

Clearly, the problems now proliferate. Parents who want to raise children who are independent and powerful may have a great deal more to do than to avoid power-playing them at home. It is not conducive to autonomy to force a child to go to a bad school no matter how cooperative the home situation. As a consequence, parents may have to choose between not sending children to the school (which means sending them to a better school which they may not be able to afford, or keeping them out of school altogether), or putting demands on the school, organizing, and becoming social activists in behalf of their children so that school becomes a better place and the child may want to go to it.

When parents have to work excessively hard or do not have the means to provide reasonable environments for their children, when families live in isolated, competitive units, each fending for its own, each desperately struggling to eat, sleep, and stay alive from day to day, there is very little opportunity to create the conditions for cooperation.

But let us imagine now a home situation which has a certain measure of ease. The parents are not overworked and underpaid. The schools are reasonable. There is enough room, food, and leisure, so that cooperation and childrearing for autonomy can be given a try.

In such a situation, the parents can work cooperatively with the children. Children can be raised reasonably free of power plays.

Children will generally conform to the wishes of their parents. They will do this out of a wish to cooperate with them because they love them, rather than out of a wish to avoid punishment or to obtain rewards. They will not *always* do as their parents wish and, at times, they will choose to do or not do what they, rather than their parents, want; but this will be accepted and understood by the parents as a reasonable price to pay for the fact that these children will be autonomous and self-sufficient, rather than dependent, passive, and powerless.

One thing is very clear, however. In a situation of this sort, children will definitely not do things that they experience as painful, obnoxious, or holding no benefit for them. Under such circumstances, children will refuse to go to bad schools, they will refuse to follow oppressive rules, they will demand to be heard when they speak, they will ask for everything that they want 100 percent of the time, and demand that their wishes be considered on an equal footing with the grown-ups in the household. Difficult as this may sound, the parents of such children have a number of rewards. First of all, they will be living with fully participating human beings. They will see the results of this in the way in which children will use their capacities to the fullest extent as they express their innate wish to cooperate. When these children grow up, they will be truly self-sufficient and autonomous and much more likely to fend for themselves and to do a good job of it; they will not tolerate injustice, oppression, lies, and exploitation. Finally, parents who choose this childrearing approach will know that their children are shaping their own destinies and following their cooperative nature, provided as they are with the freedom to choose and the tools with which to choose wisely.

Raising children in this manner is a project that cannot be undertaken in isolation. When everything in the community is decided on the basis of competitiveness and power plays it is very difficult for a specific household in that community to operate on a totally different basis. It is therefore important that people congregate in larger numbers, teach each other the principle of cooperation, start alternative schools for their children, if necessary, and support each other in their struggles to achieve a life free of Control.

What I write here is borne out in my experiences with my two children, Eric and Mimi, who are now sixteen and eighteen. For many years now, I have followed the approach outlined above with extraordinary success, as anyone who knows them will attest to.

Naturally, the theoretical position that power plays never should be used with children has its exceptions. For instance, if a baby bites its mother's nipple she has almost no choice but to power-play the child in response unless she wants to stop nursing altogether. One reasonable piece of advice is to scream loudly; this will scare the child and cause it to not bite. Screaming is a power play, but it is also a manifestation of the mother's feelings. When done with the intent of stopping the baby from biting the nipple, it is a power play but one which would be hard to argue against. Children are exposed to dangerous situations, whether it is hot stoves or sockets in the wall or busy streets. There are a few things in the child's world that the child needs to stay away from—no ifs, buts or maybes. Once again, scaring the child when it comes close to these dangerous situations is the best approach—and it is a power play; this only proves that every rule has its exceptions. But with respect to every-day matters such as when and where children sleep, what, where and when they eat, and when they get older when and where and how long they go out and whom they associate with, power plays should be avoided and replaced with emotionally literate (see p. 220) expressions of our opinions, desires, and feelings.

It takes more time to deal with a child without power plays but I believe that in the long run, children who are not power-played take less effort, less work, and stay dependent on their parents for a shorter period of time, and become self-sufficient, loving, supportive, and helpful, eventually contributing their own energy to the family. While any one situation may be more expediently dealt with by a power play, I believe that we pay dearly for every time we violate a child's rights and control it. There is no reward greater to a parent than the love of one's children and there is no better way to guarantee that children will love us than if we allow them the freedom of their choices while we provide them with our best advice, nurturing, and candid expression of our wishes and feelings.

Control at Work

The world of work is one which is traditionally organized in a hierarchical fashion. Differences in power are emphasized, and power plays are encouraged. Along with giving up Control with children, the notion of giving up Control in employment situations must seem strange to the average person who simply assumes that the workplace is by necessity a place of inequalities. People assume, also, that work will be unpleasant, joyless misery. The only way out is to start a business where they are working for themselves. Unfortunately, the likelihood of succeeding when going into business for yourself is very slim, and most small businesses fail within a year of being started, leaving the enterprising small-businessperson financially and psychologically devastated. The only benefit of going into business for oneself seems to be the rediscovery that work can be joyful when we know what we are producing, for whom we are producing it, and when the fruits of our labor return to us, rather than going to someone else.

When we hate our work, the main reason is because we are powerless. Giving the worker power at the job place is a possible goal. True, that is difficult when a business depends on the exploitation of its workers to achieve its profits. Employers believe that for survival in a competitive business world, it is necessary to squeeze as much productivity out of a worker as is possible, and this can be done only through controlling techniques, and power plays. But giving the worker power is another approach to increasing productivity; and in many employment situations, such as in civil service and government, competition is not a factor at all.

Many a workplace could be made more cooperative, less Control ridden, and more democratic, depending on how much its success depends on the exploitation of its workers. Businesses owned by the workers themselves are becoming commonplace across this country and people are learning the techniques of democratic management which give such a business a chance to succeed in the competitive marketplace. Such workplaces can bring back the joys of productive work for their workers and would seem to be an ideal alternative to self-employment.

But even if this ideal is not achieved, an employer can endeavor to treat employees in a respectful, cooperative manner, asking for their opinion and following it, sharing profits fairly, keeping controlling power plays to a minimum, and operating on an open and aboveboard basis which encourages worker participation and involvement. Early in the book, I gave an example of a workplace power play and the cooperative alternative to it. A cooperative alternative is possible in every work situation in which the employer is willing to grant his employees equal rights and human dignity, and in which an employer is unwilling to use the many tried and tested methods which employers can use to squeeze the last amount of productivity out of their employees.

13

HOW TO FILL THE CONTROL VACUUM

For me, writing a book about power seems a natural by-product of a process which started years ago—as early as 1971. I was a Ph.D. in psychology and had written a successful first book, *Games Alcoholics Play.* I was partially involved in public service, working at a free clinic, and I had a thriving private practice. I was actively involved—fighting the war in Vietnam, demonstrating, organizing, leafleting, teaching. I felt righteous and just, capable and vigorous. I was, in short, a counterculture success story: well rounded, respected, admired, alive. No one could have convinced me then that I was powerful at the expense of others and that, regarded from a certain perspective, I was a social failure.

True, I was aware of people's anger toward me (not my enemies' but my friends'), all very low-key, but nevertheless very real. But after all, I would have argued, I was a man of unusual inclinations and ideas which often bring out the insecurities of people whose own ideas are threatened. People could have pointed out my occasional but very disruptive outbursts of temper, but I would have probably dismissed these as inconsequential.

I secretly knew that I was irrationally wedded to my ideas, that I was given to falsifying the truth (lying, to be precise), and that I seldom felt love for anyone. But had anyone pointed those truths out to me, I probably would have loosed a barrage of words sufficient to silence my critic and moved to a different subject.

211

It was a woman representing womanhood in general who first brought to my awareness the subtle, daily facts of the misuse of my power. "Men oppress women," she said, and to this I handily agreed—somehow managing to exclude myself from the group of men whom I saw abusing power. The startling part of the message was, "And you, Claude, are yourself an oppressive and abusive man." I became very interested in the study of sexism and the way in which men take advantage of women. I loved women rather uncritically, and I was not going to take lightly the accusation— which I suspected to be untrue—that I was an oppressive male. I was going to investigate this matter of male oppression and prove to myself and others that I was above power abuse. Once I had demonstrated that, I could then set the matter aside: a credentialed, liberated man, above suspicion.

Becoming interested in this topic made me aware of the major tool of power abuse between human beings, the power play. It became clear that all human injustice could be easily analyzed in terms of transactional sequences which I called power plays.

Sexism was one area in which injustice became very clear to me. Men discounted women, interrupted them in the middle of their sentences, dominated them physically, manipulated them with verbal and mental tricks. I saw, more and more, to my dismay, how I myself was involved in every one of those activities. The plot began to thicken.

I realized that I was a pain in the neck not only to women, but was a member of a number of other oppressive subgroups. As a middle-aged person, I abused my power with children and older people. I was racist, I was unfair to fat people, short people. I realized that as a well-to-do professional, I oppressed, with my language and demeanor, people who had a working-class background. I began to suspect that I, a person proud to be a humanist, nevertheless had a very deep-seated and complicated inclination to use my power in ways which were not necessarily beneficial to others, and ultimately not beneficial to myself. I saw that being powerful is one thing, and how we use power is another. I soon saw, for the first time, through the urgings of others, that I was a privileged male, who was further privileged to be white, and further privileged to be educated, and further privileged to be in my middle age, and further privileged to be in a couple with a powerful woman. I also saw that all of the power I had by virtue of these privileges created responsibility, and that I was failing to act responsibly much oftener than I would have liked to admit.

I realized that my efforts at self-vindication were pointless. Power abuse was everywhere. No one was free of power abuse or sexism—no man and no woman. The point wasn't to prove myself innocent of sexism, but to understand it, find it in myself and others, and struggle against it. It was a lifetime job for myself and all the others who felt the same way. It was at this time that I became a feminist: a man who loved women, who wanted them to have their due, who wanted to find the woman in himself, and a man who would resist male supremacy, patriarchy, and power abuse in general.

With the help of friends and co-workers, who confront me lovingly, I have worked to abandon behavior which constitutes abuse of my power. My first tendency was to give up power completely, to give up my possessions, recede into oblivion, subject myself to the accusations of the angry oppressed and to the paralyzing effects of my own guilt, but I discovered very little appetite in myself for this course of action. Being powerful and abusing power are not identical; being powerful is good, abusing power is bad. I resolved to discover all of the ways in which I personally abused power, or ways in which I contributed to the abusive power of others, while keeping and using power which was not abusive.

It has been a long, arduous, joyful, at times extremely painful and bitter path. I have learned a great deal, much of it from men, most of it from women, and also from my children and old folks of my acquaintance. A great deal more remains to be learned. I have come to understand power to a sophisticated enough degree to write a book about it. I can offer myself as an example of a person who is familiar with power abuses, has used them, has had them used on himself, and has become conscious of how they harm other people, has relinquished a large number of them, and intends to continue to do so—probably for the rest of his life.

Every power abuse, except for a few bloody, violent ones, described in this book, has been part of my behavior. As a successful psychotherapist, for instance, I used my power to the hilt—and not always to my client's advantage. In my office, I sat behind a desk and in my groups, I sat on the only high-backed chair in the room, with a phone next to me, which I answered, even in the middle of the group proceedings, with a curt "Dr. Steiner." I made sure never to arrive first at meetings with my "patients" and felt no qualms when I was late for appointments at the public clinic where I worked. I tried to be more expensively and fashionably dressed, more calm and flawless—superior, in other words, to my clients.

More subtly, I interrupted, corrected, overrode, ignored, judged, evaluated, insulted, attacked, patronized, discounted, and lied to the people I worked for, I justified this by assuming that they needed my gentle, authoritative, sometimes devious, parental attitude, in order to get better. Luckily, I had enough talent and charm going for myself so that they did get better anyway; and when I began relinquishing my power abuses, they came after me with gusto. As soon as it became obvious to people in my groups that I was open to critical evaluation, the complaints started coming in, mixed in with the therapy. "Why do you seem bored?" (I decreased the number of weekly hours I worked.) "Why are you always late?" (I started arriving on time.) One day somebody was sitting in *my* chair. When I asked her to please move, she refused and asked me why I called it my chair. (Out went the chair, and eventually out went all the chairs; we now use large pillows to sit on.)

People began to complain about my tone, my superior attitude, my curt stiffness, my dogmatic pronouncements. They challenged my ideas, disagreed with me openly, discussed me after meetings, and presented me with their criticism a week later. They were much more often than not correct in their criticism, and I listened. The machine could not be stopped.

I opened myself up to these attacks and their challenge of my power abuses became an accepted part of my work, which not only improved the effectiveness of the therapy, but also taught me one valuable lesson after another. I stopped wearing ties and uncomfortable suits, I relaxed and smiled more, took more vacations, refused to raise my fees as everyone else raised them, and noticed that my clients actually seemed to love me; that they were concerned with *my* welfare, and at the same time, claimed that I was a great therapist.

To my great surprise, I seemed to gain by giving up my power abuses, whether in my work, in my love relationships, or in my relationships with friends, strangers, or even with my enemies. My healing powers actually improved as the uptight, controlling male power attitudes learned in my training were given up, one by one, and as I learned to communicate, feel and think in new ways. Finally, I felt in love in a way I never experienced before; fully, with complete commitment, without reservations, Control set aside, as my heart drank thirstily from Love's magic waters.

Putting Your Heart Back on Your Sleeve

In the previous chapter, I discussed the process whereby people who might be so inclined can give up Control power in their lives. Even for those who consider such a giving up as essential, regardless of the consequences, the question may still come up: "Now that I've given up control, is there anything left of me?" (This is a valid question. In fact, as a people give up, one after another, aspects of their controlling behavior they may find that they feel weak, small, worthless, and, in general, powerless; a feeling which can cause a great deal of alarm. This is especially true of men, who are trained to feel good when they are in Control.) We may not want to dominate other living beings, but we also don't want to be without any power whatsoever.

For some, the feeling of being small and powerless actually brings about some relief. Relief from responsibility, from guilt when we don't discharge our responsibilities, relief from having to give an impression of being powerful, in control, and successful at all times. But relief is temporary. In time, when we get used to the benefits of giving up power, the question really does come: "If not Control power, then what is there?"

The answer is that what else there is, is limitless, really. The fact that people, men especially, have focused on Control has also blinded them to other forms of power, and it is those which will be replacing Control. One particular form of power, which is the power of Love, is specifically underdeveloped and displaced by a focus on Control.

Love and Control are (as are Love and Sexuality) often confused with each other. People whose power is invested in Control characteristically lack the capacity to love. Their feelings about others have their origins in Control rather than love issues. Jealousy is a case in point.

Many people believe that jealousy is an emotion associated with love and that being jealous is an indication of how much a person loves another. Let us explore the matter of jealousy, as an occasion to distinguish between Control and Love.

The fact that a person wants another does not necessarily mean that there is any love involved. People often want others in the same way they want a car, a house, or any other kind of property. Very often, wanting someone simply indicates the desire to possess and control, a desire which comes from a different source from the source of Love. Yet, the confusion is real and the differences are difficult to ascertain. Feelings of Love and Control can be mixed together so that any one object or person can bring out both in someone, so that it isn't clear just what is going on. It is in the case of jealousy, when the object or person is taken away from us, that we sometimes get a very clear-cut basis for the difference.

I own a 1952 GMC truck which I have worked over many times and which I know as intimately as I know some people. When I sit in my truck, I have a feeling very similar to love for it. People sometimes react to other human beings in the same way I react to my truck and have no hesitation to call their feelings Love. This is a common mistake; one for which people who live in a society totally dominated by ideas of private ownership can hardly be blamed.

The basic Control relationship occurs between a person and an object. The attachment felt by the person has to do with physical, visible, material dimensions of the object of Control. When we control an object, we want to be able to use it whenever needed, we want to preserve its newness and its originality, we want in short, to own it as our private property. This implies that we have sole, unlimited access to it, that we can dispose of it, use it or not use it, trade it or sell it at will. Consequently we do not recognize any particular rights that the object might have. And yet we can develop feelings of fondness and affection for it, as I have for my truck. Such feelings are commonly experienced by men (and women, too, of course) about animals, slaves, employees, women, land, trees, and other property.

Perhaps the best way to describe the difference between Love and Control is that love is experienced as a connection, a bond, a mutual attraction, a desire to be with, an awareness as vivid and clear of what the other being feels and experiences as of one's own feelings and experiences. Because the focus of Love is not exclusively in ourselves, but is the result of a reciprocal flow, it really cannot be said that we love a piece of steel or some other inanimate object. All of this may be taken to mean that jealousy is just a manifestation of our need to Control others, but this is not always necessarily so. There are, in my mind, two forms of jealousy.

CONTROL JEALOUSY

When jealousy has to do with possessiveness—the desire to dominate the other person's movements—it is connected to primitive, territorial possessive instincts which are applied to objects as well as people. The desire that some people have to define their private property and to exercise control over it manifest itself in this form of jealousy. In feeling this kind of jealousy, we don't care about the circumstances or details or consider the other person's emotional needs. We simply are unwilling and incapable of accepting the loss of control over an object. We may not even love or care about that person. We may be ourselves involved with second, third, and fourth lovers, but we regard that person as our property and, just as I wouldn't accept a stranger's driving away in my truck, we are unable to accept our partners' freedom and right to their own choices. Control jealousy has nothing to do with Love, though it is often mistaken for it.

DEFICIT JEALOUSY

A second form of jealousy has to do with a sense of unfair exchange. When people enter into relationships with each other, they quite naturally offer each other love, nurture, support, physical and material benefits—all without particularly discussing the terms of the exchange, but assuming or hoping that the exchange will be fair.

Let us say that one takes part of the exchange, withdraws it from the relationship, and gives it to somebody else. Jealousy may reasonably ensue. This is not a matter of possessiveness, but of a violation of an agreement for exchange which leaves one of the parties unfairly treated.

Maybe the relationship between Jill and Jack is one in which a great deal of inequity already exists. Typically, Jill may be giving Jack a lot of nurturing and strokes in exchange for which she gets very little—except a man to call her own. If Jack then proceeds to apply some of his stingily given strokes to someone else, Jill may experience a tremendous amount of jealousy that has to do with an injured sense of fairness, which throws into question how valid the loving relationship between Jack and Jill really is. This type of jealousy is not related to Control but to the mutuality of the Love between the two people.

If there was such a thing as pure Love, it would completely exclude Control. Giving up Control affords us the opportunity to learn how to Love because having disposed of our desire to control any one thing or person, we can then see what Love there is in our hearts by seeing what remains.

I hope I have successfully illustrated how the pain of unreciprocated love is often confused with the pain we feel when we are not able to Control others. They feel similar, but they're different. The distinction between them is useful for those who want to abandon Control and pursue Love in their lives.

The ultimate reward for giving up Control is the rediscovery of Love. Yet, a person giving up Control power will not necessarily immediately develop the capacity to love. In fact, the development of the power of Love is going to need to be preceded by a number of other developments.

The first of these developments is a phenomenon that seems to occur anytime that we withdraw from a source of powerful stimulation such as our addiction to Control really is. I first noticed this when working with alcoholics who developed withdrawal panic a week or so after they stopped drinking. This panic usually lasts for months, until the vacuum left by the alcohol is filled with new forms of activity and stimulation.

The same kind of panic is felt by people giving up Control; once our hold loosens, Control tends to give way precipitously, and depression and anxiety are prone to follow while the emotional literacy skills required for a full emotional life develop. It also takes a while for people to notice the change: some will like it, some will not. But the rewards and appreciation from other people will take some time before materializing and that period of time, that hiatus between Control and the Other Side of Power, can be a trying rite of passage and can test our resolve.

Emotional Literacy

Emotional literacy is a dimension of our personalities which is badly neglected as long as we are invested in being powerful through the avenue of Control.

Excessive focus on the intricacies of Control behavior displaces awareness of a proper understanding of, and relationship with, our emotions. In order to Control people, we have to control their emotions because emotions are the source of inner-directedness, autonomous acts, and unpredictable behavior. People who Control others need also to keep their own emotions under control. In fact, being a Controlling person implies cold-bloodedness, lack of feelings for one's fellows. Control requires that emotions be disregarded and oppressed out of existence. *Kaltblutigheit* (cold-bloodedness) was the most useful attribute for the bureaucrats of Nazi mass murder; the ultimate, monstrous, manifestation of Control gone totally out of control.

Emotional literacy is an important aspect of the Other Side of Power. It liberates the power and understanding of our and others' emotions. It is a skill which we should absorb from our parents or other grown-ups around us when we are small. Unfortunately many of us don't, so that we must learn it as adults. Emotional literacy spells the difference between a humanoid competitive mechanism and a fully alive, aware, and loving human being.

Let me explain. The realm of our feelings is a vast unexplored area for most of us. This world, which many of us avoid, is like a jungle inhabited by dangerous, wild animals, which we would rather pretend is not within us or others.

I once had a dream in which I was living in one of those suburban houses with a kitchen which led to a back yard. I was in the kitchen and the curtains to the back yard were drawn. I knew that there was something in the back yard which I was afraid of facing. I could hear wild jungle noises, the grunts of animals, the slithering of snakes, the dripping of jungle moisture, the rushing of torrential waters. I felt safe in the house. There seemed to be no need for me to go into the back yard, nor any danger that what was going on in the back yard would intrude into the kitchen. However, I felt an intense fascination by what was going on behind the door. I tried to ignore those goings on and go along about my business but was unable to do so internally though I quite successfully pretended externally.

If I as much as cracked the door, a blast of jungle air and noise caused me to slam the door shut in great panic. There the dream ends. But when I awoke and thought about it I realized that here I was, like Alice in Wonderland, on the wrong side of the door looking through the keyhole of the world of my emotional insides. We take occasional peeks through the door of our defenses into the wondrous realm of our emotions where Control has no sway. As long as we stay on this side of the door we may feel safe, but we are cold, alone, and afraid.

All of us are, to one extent or another, emotionally illiterate, and the degree of illiteracy can be likened to a squelch mechanism exactly like the one which operates in a citizens'-band radio. The squelch can be set very low, in which case all of the transmissions—whether loud or very faint—can be heard. Or it can be high, so that only the loudest gets through. Figure A shows a sequence of feelings and their intensity throughout one day. Figure B shows what the person actually experiences when the feelings are squelched. Everything below the squelch line is blotted out

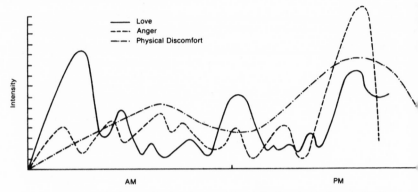

Figure 1A A Graphic Display of Some of Jack's Feelings in the Course of a Day

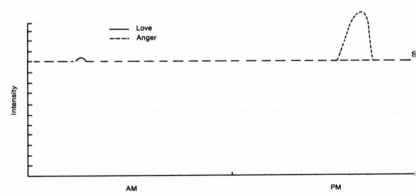

Figure 1B The Squelching of Feelings and the Resulting Contents of Consciousness

of awareness. Figure 1A traces three of the many feelings Jack experiences in one day—love, anger, physical discomfort—are fluctuating. Yet, when feelings are squelched to a certain level of intensity, all that the person is aware of is a small feeling of love in the morning and a burst of anger in the evening. All other feelings at all other times are buried.

Some people are emotionally literate and can "read" and understand the subtle language of the body, in themselves and others. Other people cannot; their own feelings often go unperceived and when they are noticed, are unclear and muddled; only their most blatant feelings are understood, and the feelings of others are similarly unclear and forgotten. Some simply feel that emotions are unnecessary, self-indulgent, and even stupid.

If we should suddenly become tuned in to the events within our skins, we would become aware of a large number of happenings, many of which we would find frightening, unacceptable, bizarre, and often amazing. People who are (for better or for worse) tuned in to the subtleties of their bodily experiences and who incautiously speak of them or act on them at the wrong time, in the wrong place, are in grave danger of being considered insane. We are wise not to speak too freely of the energies that travel through our bodies, of the fantasies that go on in our day- or sleeping dreams, of the sensations we feel in our hands and limbs, heads, hearts, and bellies, of the kinds of things that really give us pleasure or pain, of our real feelings.

The "normal" unfeeling experience is one of emptiness, vacuum, joylessness; it leaves us unexplainably and deeply dissatisfied. To fill the void, we seek stimulation which is strong and capable of breaking through the barrier. We find strong stimulation in fast-paced, loud music, violence, speeding, pornography, overeating, spending money; and, above all, we find it in drugs. Drugs punch through the Control barrier and temporarily reestablish contact with the bodily experience. Unfortunately, the contact is brief, followed by the harmful and painful aftereffects of the drug.

Then the barrier goes up again, only to be brought down again by larger doses of the drug.

People's reactions to the realm of their feelings reminds me of the way people feel about snakes. In the mountains where I live, rattlesnakes abound in the summer. Anyone who does not treat that fact with respect is taking a chance. Yet rattlesnakes are beautiful animals which never attack anyone without provocation, which are most often seen slithering away, and, if threatened, will give you ample warning with a distinctive shake of their rattle.

One option we have, when the summer comes, is to live in fear of rattlesnakes, to wish to kill each one we see and to try to cleanse the countryside of them. The other option is to be aware of their presence and incorporate them into our daily consciousness, to coexist with them, avoid cornering or stepping on them, and, if they come too close for comfort, pick them up and move them a safe distance away and appreciate their magnificent beauty and significance in our lives. It is not by chance that it was the serpent that conveyed the apple to Adam and Eve, for the serpent does represent the emotions and has been from early patriarchial religion considered an evil animal which, like the emotions, is to be destroyed.

Emotional literacy seeks to lead us to consciously coexist with our emotions and reenter that jungle paradise which they guard: the realm of the Other Side of Power. In this realm, we behold the beauty of our humanness, the fragility of life, the vibrant colors and smells of nature, the miracles of seed germination and growth, the wondrous cycles of birth and death, all of which are hidden from view by our obsession and addiction to Control.

Emotional literacy is a powerful awareness which replaces Control power. Being emotionally literate, we are able to relate effectively, cooperatively, lovingly, nurturingly with other people and get what we need and want without oppressing others. Emotional literacy makes us aware of the ugliness of lies, the unfairness of discounts, the importance of emotions—good and bad, ours and others. Emotional literacy teaches us about Love and Hate, intuition and paranoia, the difference between thoughts and emotions, and how to use both together to give us power in the world.

Intuition and Love

Intuition—the capacity of knowing without identifiable information—is often underdeveloped in people. It is an important component of a full, loving response because without it we can't really know how other people feel. Without intuition, mutuality is most difficult and enduring love impossible. Intuition is a way of knowing which is not often recognized as having any real basis. Still it exists, and it is available to all people. It is particularly underdeveloped in people who pride themselves on being rational and who want to know what they know based on discrete observable facts, which are combined according to the rules of logic. The vague, unformed, inexplicable way in which intuition makes itself manifest is not attended to by most men, who often think of it as a form of feminine irrationality. The fact is, however, that intuition combined with reason gives a person access to expanded knowledge, which is a great improvement over reason (or intuition) alone.

In *A Separate Reality,* Carlos Castaneda quite rationally argues against Don Juan's claim that it is possible to avoid dangerous situations, really:

> "It is not possible to live strategically all the time. Imagine that someone is waiting for you with a powerful rifle with a telescopic sight; he could spot you accurately five hundred yards away. What would you do?"
>
> Don Juan looked at me with an air of disbelief and then broke into laughter.
>
> "What would you do?" I urged him.

"If someone is waiting for me with a rifle with a telescopic sight?" he said, obviously mocking me.

"If someone is hiding out of sight, waiting for you. You won't have a chance. You can't stop a bullet."

"No, I can't. But I still don't understand your point."

"My point is that all your strategy cannot be of any help in a situation like that."

"Oh, but it can. If someone is waiting for me with a powerful rifle with a telescopic sight, I simply will not come around."

Interestingly, the development of intuition is effectively pursued through the validation of paranoia. The reason for this, as I have explained elsewhere,[47] is that paranoia is the result of the suppression of intuition. In *The Politics of the Family,* R. D. Laing points out that people's experiences of the world are continually being invalidated and forcibly replaced by the "official" view of events. He speaks of a woman whose experience is that, though she is officially married (with a certificate and a wedding ceremony to prove the fact), her "husband" is in fact not married to her at all; his behavior belies any marital agreement. He shows no love, respect, or interest in her. When she claims that he is not her husband, she is taken to a psychiatrist; her experience (he is not her husband) is invalidated. This invalidation, when it takes an extreme form, sometimes turns people into mental invalids gone mad with what the psychiatric establishment calls paranoid schizophrenia. When we notice what goes on with other people, and these perceptions are denied or discounted, we are basically squelching our intuitive powers. When the unpleasant facts of life are denied, the result (for most of us who don't go mad) is that we develop the kinds of nagging and repetitive suspicions and misgivings which are our common, garden-variety, everyday paranoias.

Paranoia is heightened awareness. This statement, which I first made in 1969 in the Radical Psychiatry Manifesto, was at the time seen as an outrageous notion even by myself. It was designed to reassure myself and others in the antiwar movement that our paranoia about Nixon, the FBI, and the CIA were valid. Today we all know that our suspicions were more than valid; in fact, what was really going on was worse than some of us ever imagined and probably remains undiscovered.

Intuition is our capacity to know beyond what our senses tell us. We know the world through our eyes and ears, touch and smell. But we have what is called a "sixth sense"—intuition—through which knowledge about the world is available as well. When that knowledge is denied, some of us become paranoid.

Paranoia is the last vestige of our intuition, denied. Some of us have been so browbeaten by the scientific way of thinking and have taken so seriously the denials of all of what we experience intuitively, that we do not even have any paranoia left. There are two kinds of truly insane people: those who think *everyone* is after them, and those who think *no one* is after them. Both of these are relatively rare and it turns out that almost everyone, if they search their consciousness carefully, will find, in some hidden, dark corner of their mind, that they are in fact harboring some invalidated suspicions. It is to this last remaining glimmer of our lost intuition that we need to attach ourselves; it will be the touchstone, the first building step of our intuitive powers.

For example, let us say that Joe is a friend of yours and that you develop an intuition that he is angry at you. In fact, he is not really angry, but every time he comes into your house, he does feel a pang of envy about the fact that you have many things he wants but cannot afford. He is embarrassed about his feelings and assumes that if you knew about them you would feel threatened. You slowly develop a notion that something is wrong, but you know that if you were to broach this subject with him, he would deny it. This is, of course, the very reason why your intuition has not been able to develop: because people hide their feelings from you. In order to cultivate your intuition, it will be necessary that you strike up or develop cooperative relationships in which the mutual sharing, discussion, and checking out of intuitions and paranoid fantasies is a real possibility. Relationships that are based on control depend very heavily on deception, double-dealing, and masking of emotions. In these relationships, it is not very likely that people would be willing to confirm or validate any particular intuition that you might have. In order to learn intuition, you will have to find people who are willing to share their innermost feelings freely.

Given that you reach an understanding with Joe that you and he will talk about each other's intuitions whenever necessary, it will be possible for both of you to pursue your intuitive powers actively by checking them against reality and, with the aid of this feedback, correct, develop, and sharpen them. The validation of your paranoia about Joe might proceed as follows.

"Joe, I have a feeling (paranoia) to check with you. Would you be willing to listen to it?"

"Okay, let's hear it."

"Whenever you come to my house, I have the feeling that you are angry at me. Sometimes I think you're angry at me for having so many expensive things."

Joe thinks about this, and even though it does not seem at all true to begin with, he carefully searches for a grain of truth that may be the cause for your feelings.

"Well, I don't think that I am angry because you have so many things. In fact, I believe they would be a burden. But I do feel some envy which I am not proud of. I am a little bit annoyed with you for not offering to let me drive your car when I need transportation. Maybe that's what you are picking up."

"I see, that makes sense. It could explain how I feel . . .

Well, I'll think about your driving my car. I think it really would be nice if you could drive it. I'm just worried that you'll scratch the new paint, but I believe that you would probably take good care of it and I would enjoy sharing it with you."

In the above process, you first share your crude, intuitive perception with Joe, who separates the part of it that is not true from the part that is true, thereby giving you an opportunity to see where your intuition is accurate and where it is inaccurate.

This kind of feedback will make it much easier for you to understand Joe in the future, and it is a learning experience in intuition. A series of such validations is a most effective way of refining one's intuitive processes and one's emotional literacy. This is admittedly a very simplified instance; there are a great number of situations in which feelings, running under the surface of relationships, become the object of a person's intuition. Marked feelings of affection, love, envy, anger, happiness, unhappiness, rejection, dejection, jealousy, are going on in people all the time. And for a person who is an intuitive perceiver, all of those feelings are as real as whatever is being manifested in a more overt way. As these intuitive perceptions become clearer and more subject to awareness, they become a part of the person's reality. People who are intuitive, therefore, live in a different world of reality from people who are not. The gap between their experiences is, at times, quite large. For instance, in a conversation, some people (and this is true, generally, of men) hear only the words which are spoken. Others will hear tones and inflections, reflecting feelings of anxiety, certainty, fear, hope. When these two sorts of people listen to a third, their experiences can be completely different. When they speak to each other, their lack of communication can be mind-boggling.

Intuitive knowledge can vary in its intensity and its accuracy. Sometimes we have vague intuitions which are not very accurate; sometimes we have strong, inescapable perceptions, which are so obvious as to be unavoidably true. It is important to recognize that intuition is not as exact as the kind of knowledge which we derive from measuring something with a yardstick, or some other measuring device. Therefore we need to judge the reliability of what we intuit, so that we don't overreact or underreact to our intuitive perceptions.

The sophisticated use of intuition includes a number of factors. Suppose, for instance, that you are going to a gathering of people, all of whom are working together to bring about an important political end—say, the establishment of a committee to elect a city councilperson. At that gathering you meet a number of different new people, all of whom may be seriously involved in the campaign. One of the newcomers, Cindy, is a likable enough person, but gives you a strong feeling that she is getting involved for unclear reasons. You seem to feel that her interest is one of anger toward the other candidate, rather than one of genuine interest and desire to promote the political aims of your group.

At a certain point, Cindy offers to become the treasurer of the group. Carl, who is not as energetic, but gives you a better feeling, is willing to serve in the same capacity. It would seem that judging from Cindy's overt energy, she would be the best candidate for the job, yet your intuition tells you that you don't want her. The sense of the others is that they are willing to support Cindy, but you state why you like Carl for the job. Your statement somewhat crystallizes in others the same feelings that you have had, questions are asked of Cindy about her schedule and her commitment, and the group decides for Carl, who accepts willingly. A few weeks later, Cindy stop coming to the committee's meetings, proving that her interest was probably not as thorough and intense as it might have seemed to begin with. By using your intuitive perception, you made a decision which might vitally and fundamentally affect the course of the committee's work, and perhaps the election of your candidate, and eventually the quality of life in your city.

This is an instance of giving intuitive information the proper weight and using it with good timing. Had you ignored it when you first had it, you might have had to struggle long and hard later. On the other hand, you did not overreact. Your timely support for Carl and questions to Cindy were sufficient, to quietly, almost uneventfully, turn the tide. Had the others not shared your feeling, you would have been outvoted. This is the subtle power of the properly timed use of intuition.

One payoff of the development of one's power of intuition is the heightened capacity to know and understand our loved ones. Two people who develop a finely tuned knowledge of each other's emotional lives, whether they be spouses, friends, parent and child, or siblings, can have the possibility of experiencing the kind of mutuality, concern, joy of each other's pleasures and sharing of each other's griefs and tribulations, and consequent harmony undisturbed by misunderstanding and discord which makes being human truly worthwhile.

The fear of emotional literacy and heightened intuition has its roots partially in the fact that as we become aware of our and others' feelings we also become subject to fear and grief. I know that when I began to consider opening up my awareness to my and other people's emotions I was occasionally suddenly frightened when I realized how the connections I was making were exposing me to pain and shock in a way which I had never allowed before.

I asked myself: do I want to open myself up to the vulnerabity that will be the consequence? Will I be able to stand the pain of losing a person I have come to love deeply? How will I deal with death, sickness, financial catastrophes, or need? When seen in that light, it seemed that it would have been better to stay in my isolated bubble, unaware of the deep pain that I was making myself liable to.

Yet on balance there is no question that at least in the present circumstances in which I live there is more joy than grief in being open to and aware of the feelings inside and outside of me. I can imagine circumstances of widespread human misery where it would be advantageous for the sake of self-preservation to disconnect and stop one's intuitions from functioning so as to become invulnerable to the surrounding pain.

Let us hope that we will not be afflicted by such disasters. I firmly believe that it is widespread emotional literacy that will help us preserve a world in which the balance sheet is weighed on the side of joy rather than grief.

Giving Up Control Adds Life

Giving up Control affects the whole person, psychologically as well as physically. The state of body and mind which accompanies being fixated on Control power is one of tension. The person has to be constantly vigilant not to lose Control over himself or others and generally assumes a great deal of responsibility for far too many things. The concentration on specific issues of Control will cause her to lose sight on the effect her behavior has on her own body. This disregard will generalize and manifest itself in an overall disconnection from her own bodily feelings and sensations. The constant state of anxiety and vigilance with regard to external situations will make it literally impossible to notice what she is experiencing. She will neglect the signals of impending disease, of overexertion, of chronic fatigue, of malnutrition, whether it be from eating too much, or too little. In short it will make her unaware of both the pleasures and the pain that she is feeling throughout her life. Giving up control brings about an intensification of one's awareness of the internal processes of the body. As a person gives up control, he is likely to become more interested in what he eats, how he feels, whether he is doing an inadequate amount of exercise, and whether he is holding a painful amount of tension anywhere in his body.

A whole new set of concerns will develop related to his physical integrity. His diet, sleeping, and exercise habits are likely to change and readjust to more healthy patterns. In turn, this will affect how he relates to other people.

People who are in control tend to avoid situations in which they experience feelings of powerlessness, loss, hurt, impotent anger, jealousy, and in general all of the feelings which accompany situations in which one is one-down and not in control.

When I began to give up Control, I felt, for the first time in my life, jealousy of an incredibly intense sort (I had thought I was not jealous), loneliness, incapacity to "manage" my feelings, and the rage that controlling people feel when they can't get what they want from another person. I experienced all of these in connection with a relationship that did not go in the direction in which I wanted it to go, an unusual experience for me until that time. I went through a prolonged period of unpleasant one-down feelings which other people in my life had often experienced in relation to me. The shoe was, as it were, on the other foot, and for the first time I really understood certain experiences which I had never allowed myself to have before, because I had always kept Control of myself in relationships. This was an important aspect of learning intuition.

Right alongside the negative emotions which I brought upon myself by giving up Control, there was a set of positive feelings which were also new to me. I became more loving, more capable of communicating with people, softer, more compassionate, more thoughtful and meditative—a more pleasant and pleasurable human being. At the same time, my attachment to material things diminished, and my life was less dominated and driven by sexual considerations as well. I noticed an increased amount of affection and loving feelings coming to me from other people wherever I went, and a capacity to respond to people's feelings with similar feelings of my own.

Relationships Between Men

For a man, one of the inevitable consequences of giving up Control is that his relationships with other men will change. The relationships between men, though they may seem to vary considerably among different individuals, all seem to have one quality in common. Regardless of the amount of cordiality and friendliness that may be exchanged among them, the impervious layer, the rock bottom, the impenetrable barrier seems to be that men do not touch each other. Sure, men will allow their hands to make contact with another man's body, especially through clothing, or if the touch is quick and more like a pat or a hit. Men will squeeze each other's hands in a handshake, and men will appear to touch each other on occasion, and some even frequently. But this physical contact is very deceptive. If it is compared in duration and intensity with the kinds of physical contact that men pursue and maintain with women, it will be seen that there is an enormous difference, which is very telling about the contact that men have with each other. Men simply do not feel comfortable with each other's physical touch, unless it is in contact sports. They will keep a wider gap between themselves and other men than they will between themselves and women, and they will make actual physical contact shorter and less frequent. With respect to the unseen energy flow that cannot, for the moment, be measured between human beings, I would say, from having observed many men, including myself, that there are extremely large barriers to warmth and intimacy between men. (Obviously, I am speaking here of heterosexual men.)

The reason for this is that men have a knee-jerk competitive response toward each other. A competitive response assumes that one needs to control one's own responses in order not to give up the one-up advantage with respect to another. The kind of wary vigilance which is involved in measuring out one's territory, making sure that it isn't intruded upon, defeating one's position, does not make for warmth and closeness. In addition, the physical and sexual phobias that men feel with respect to other men neatly paint men into a corner when it comes to relating to each other.

One of the exercises that developed early in the feminist consciousness movement which was effective in making men aware of their sexism was to have them reverse roles with women, as I described earlier in Chapter 12. But, if one wants to understand how sexism affects men's relationships to other men, then the exercise to do is one in which a group of men all pretend to be women. In this exercise, men will attempt to behave toward each other the way women do. Through this exercise, men become intensely aware of the obstacles in their relationships with other men. Yet it also becomes clear, as the exercise progresses, that these obstacles are not based on some inherent emotional lack, but on the prohibitions and fears which are so universally maintained by men.

Men—and I count myself among them—are afraid of other men. They're afraid of their competitiveness. They're afraid of their violence. They're afraid of their lack of emotional involvement. But, as human beings, men do not really like to compete, they really don't like violence, and they want to be emotionally involved. Where do they turn for cooperation, gentleness, and emotional involvement? They turn to women, of course. And why shouldn't men turn to women for those things? After all, that is what women are there for, aren't they? I've heard it said by men that they prefer to relate to women because women are simply more likable, more pleasant to be with, more enjoyable than men—who are, as a rule, not that interesting. Why go looking for the kinds of things that we want from people who don't really have them for us?

What are the benefits of relating to men? Men have qualities which other men like and which women don't have. Men are different from women. Perhaps this is due only to their upbringing, their sex-role training—but it could also be that they are different for more fundamental, biologically based reasons. Men are usually stronger, harder. Their interests run along certain lines. Their emotions are channeled in certain ways. Whether these differences are innate or acquired, they nevertheless exist and do not always reflect negative qualities.

It's very difficult to explain the satisfaction that is felt when relating to a person who in his total overall response presents a hard, strong surface, steadier, less vulnerable, easier to lean and rely on. It's a different feeling from what is felt when relating to a woman. It is not a better feeling—just different, and satisfying in its own way.

You may have noticed that I have a "thing" about cars and machines. I find that men share my love of machines in a way seldom found in women, and that is a source of pleasure for me. It is good to find the similarity of thinking and feeling and experiences which exists between men. It is good to relate to one who is like oneself and who understands, as no woman really can, what it is like to be a man. This will be true as long as men and women are as different as they are, for whatever reason. It is difficult for me to paint a picture of what it is like since the experience is one that creates strong emotions in me, but I know that men find it profoundly satisfying when they can share their kinship with men. In a way, we have to take it on faith that our relationships with each other are worthy of pursuit. It's a fearful, dark mystery, what we have for each other, yet my heart leaps with anticipation when I let myself think about it. The development of brotherhood among men is one of the hidden premises of feminism. I look forward to a world where men can relate to each other lovingly and with trust instead of with competitive, coldness, hate, and fear.

Giving up Control and issuing into the Other Side of

Power is equivalent to joining the human race. As we do, we discover that we are not alone, that there are countless others, wherever we go, unseen by Control's cold eye, who are themselves intensely involved in the race for survival of our humanness. We need only lift our heads to see somebody always within reach of our hands whose sparkle will meet our eye:

> Yes, I see you, sister
> Yes, I touch you, brother
> Yes, I feel you, child
> Like the web of a spider
> Seen by the searching eye
> We are connected
> Heart to Heart
> Mind to Mind
> Hand to Hand
>   We will prevail!

CODA

Mary

When John and Mary met, Mary had been divorced for two years after an eight-year marriage and was living alone with her two children. She felt reasonably secure and strong, working at her job and making ends meet, but she found herself bone weary, at times, doing it all alone. She sought friendships, with the hope that they would be intimate, which might make life less lonely, more joyful, less hard. She was no sexual prude, but had, in the last year, refused the sexual intimacies offered to her by men, because she concluded that by and large, casual sex that had no promise of developing into an intimate relationship, and, even though enjoyable, was likely, for her, to be a source of more pain than pleasure. She had developed a number of satisfying friendships with men and women which nourished her but, nevertheless, it was quite clear that she wanted a more intimate relationship in which she could give in to her emotional needs and in which she could practice the emotional skills that she was learning in the therapy group she attended weekly. It was not clear to her what kind of person she was looking for, whether older, younger, male or female—she just knew she needed someone closer but she also knew that no matter how urgent the need, she was not going to compromise herself. After spending her twenties in a most commonplace and unsatisfactory marriage, she wanted to turn over a new leaf. She wanted, more than anything, equality. Equality in child care, in income-earning work, in emotional exchange, and especially, equality of commitment. In her marriage, which she struggled long and hard to preserve, she had always felt that he didn't care nearly as much as she did. When she finally asked for a divorce, her husband stunned her by seeming to have no objections or regrets except for the economic ones of splitting up the property.

Learning about emotional literacy, power, and power plays in her problem-solving therapy group illuminated what had happened in her marriage. They both had lied, mostly by omission; they had not shared responsibilities fairly; they hadn't asked for what they wanted or said how they felt. He had plagued her endlessly, largely successfully, to get what he wanted: her warmth and nurturing support. She had power-played him, largely unsuccessfully, to get him to listen to her, talk to her, become committed.

Never again: she was resolute. Yet she was afraid that her high expectations would never be fulfilled. Men just did not seem interested in a divorced mother of two, in her thirties, who wanted equal rights to boot.

Consequently, she was surprised when, just hours after meeting John at one of her friend's parties, she found herself in his car driving home and looking forward to the night's end when she hopefully, expectantly, visualized making love to him. She felt a very strong, surprising attraction, not just sexual, but a pull which tugged at her like tiny invisible fibers. She knew enough to realize that this feeling was one-sided, self-generated, and highly volatile, but there was something about him that was different. It had to do with eye contact, with a certain solicitous thoughtfulness and curiosity, and with several statements that he had made which quite unmistakably defined him as being sympathetic to women's issues, pro-ERA, a potential feminist.

They met over the buffet table, and a casual comment about dry crackers had led to a dazzling conversation, topics strung one after the other, like pearls on a string. They had talked non-stop, all smiles and excitement, but as they drove to John's house, she was suddenly wary, afraid; her insides grew cold. She remembered similar excitement before, and how it had ended. She tried to shake the feeling, but John seemed to notice because he looked at her, and asked, "Is something wrong?"

She looked back at him with surprise.

"Why do you ask?"

"It's just that I suddenly noticed a change in you, like a cloud over a sunny sky."

Mary remembered her emotional literacy lessons: "Say what you feel. Ask for what you want. Don't power-play." Her tendency was to lie, dismiss her sudden fear, and go on trying to recapture the multicolored bird of her passion. But her lessons came back: "Say what you feel." "Ask for what you want." She realized she would have to tell John how excited she was and she was afraid of revealing too much, giving too much away, losing her power. Nevertheless, she said, "I suddenly was afraid because I am too excited, too much anticipating."

John eased the car into a parking spot on the busy street on which they were driving, and faced her.

"What are you afraid of?"

"I'll tell you what I am afraid of, if you tell me how you feel. Are you excited? Are you feeling passionate?"

"I haven't really stopped to think about it, but now that I do, I think I could be afraid of the same thing you are. I am worried that we will have a wonderful time and that you'll be too excited, and that you'll cling, grow dependent, and that I will be trapped by your emotions. But I don't want to think about such negativity and neither should you. Why don't we just go ahead and enjoy ourselves?"

Mary was silent for a long time. John waited for her response. She felt warmed by his silence, his willingness to wait for her to think and to form an opinion. So often in such situations with a man, her experience had been to receive a torrent of words from him which temporarily overwhelmed her doubts.

Finally she said, "I appreciate you giving me time to

think about this. Look, John, I'm not interested in doing this thing thoughtlessly; I want it to be good, I want it to remain good. I think you are very sexy. I don't want to overreact, I don't want to cling, I don't want to become dependent, and I don't want you to ignore your feelings or mine."

As soon as she finished speaking it seemed to Mary that she had committed a grave mistake. That marvelous flow, that excitement seemed to have stopped, in a logjam of emotions. She blamed herself and her obsession with analyzing emotional issues, which according to her husband had ruined their marriage. She was considering some kind of an apologetic gesture, when John responded,

"I know what you are saying. I'm interested. I realize that it is important. I have a lot to learn."

They didn't have sex that evening, but they did go to John's house and lay around on the couch and after agonizing over whether she should wake up her girlfriend at whose house her children were staying, she decided to do so and stay the night. Eventually they went to bed. Something in Mary caused her to ask to postpone what both of them very badly wanted, so they talked and slept fitfully. Several times during the night she woke up and felt good lying next to him, but then she worried that she wasn't getting a good night's sleep and that she'd be tired the next day.

At those times she realized that even if she wanted to go home she was stranded without a car. Next time she'd bring her own transportation. This time she would just relax and enjoy the feeling of sleeping with another person. She was glad they hadn't had sex earlier and now she felt wonderfully attracted to John. She considered waking him up, but didn't.

They finally had sex several dates later; it was glorious according to Mary, spectacular according to John. In the meantime they had discussed their respective wishes for relationships and what they wanted from each other. John had another lover, Karla, a woman who was married and who with her husband's consent wanted to maintain a light-hearted sexual friendship with him. He liked Mary a great deal, but he was not prepared to give up his relationship with Karla. He wanted to know Mary better and spend time with her. He found her extremely attractive and desirable and was especially interested in her knowledge about feminism and emotional literacy.

Mary wasn't sure how she felt about John's relationship with Karla. It immediately caused her to want to pursue another lover to even things out, but she realized that that was only a defensive maneuver, a power play if you will, to see whether she could get John to give up Karla. She decided that as long as she felt he was being a positive influence in her life, taking care of her needs, and as long as things were good, she would stay with John anyway.

Mary was especially pleased by John's response to her children. He too had been married and had a child of his own, and he was not interested in having another child; he missed his daughter who was living with his wife across the country and whom he only saw for brief periods of time during school vacations. Mary had feared that like the other men in her experience he would be uninterested in her children and in her because of them. But instead he took a real liking to them, especially Kay, her six-year-old, the older of the two children.

Above all, Mary and John were both extremely attracted to the notions of a cooperative relationship, one which operates without power plays, or secrets and one in which people do their equal share and don't do things they don't want to do. It seemed to both of them that they were ready for such a relationship, even though they did not know whether they could actually accomplish it. Consequently, John was eager to hear from Mary what she was learning about cooperative relationships in her problem-solving group.

John was something of a loner, absorbed in his work. He enjoyed meeting Mary's circle of friends. Mary's friends were involved in various cooperative ventures such as a care center and school, and a food store. All of these people, though different in many ways, had in common a desire to live in an environment of cooperation, free of the hierarchies and power plays of which they had grown tired over the years. John and Mary attended the occasional potluck dinners and parties with the people who participated in the network of cooperative activities in their town. He was surprised to find that there was an active subculture of people who all shared basic cooperative ideals and who knew each other and were each other's friends.

After six months of spending much time together John and Mary decided that they would like at least to move closer since they lived 30 minutes away from each other at opposite ends of town. John had been spending most of his time at Mary's house because of her children, but he was dissatisfied with this arrangement and all the driving he had to do. Mary wanted to spend time with him at his place as well, but again, it was too far. They discussed moving in together but felt that this was not exactly what they wanted either. They did not relish the thought of what seemed to be another marriage so soon after their divorces. They had fallen in love and were rapidly coming to love each other as well but were not ready to commit themselves to that kind of nuclear family arrangement at this point, if ever. On the other hand, it was obvious that it would be economically advantageous to live under the same roof. The rent could be shared, driving would be reduced, much needed money could be used for other purposes.

They discussed their quandary with their friends, asking for ideas about what to do. One of their friends referred them to Clancy, who owned a very large house in which she had recently been living with several people. She might be interested in living with the two of them and Mary's children. The rent would be much cheaper than two separate apartments or houses and yet they would not be in the kind of confined, isolated situation that is usually associated with living under the same roof. John and Mary thought this over, met Clancy, and looked the house over. They could each have a room for themselves and the children could have their own room next to Clancy's son, Eric. They would have the privacy that they needed. They enjoyed the idea of eating meals with the others in the house—wondered what they would do if they ever wanted to eat by themselves or wanted real privacy. When the economics of the situation were thoroughly examined, it was clear that it was worth a try. Kevin, Mary's son, knew Clancy's son, Eric, from school and liked the idea of living with him; Kay was not so sure but she liked the idea of living with John. The house was in a beautiful location, a good neighborhood, close to the school, so John and Mary approached Clancy's household for admission. A meeting with everyone was arranged—Clancy, her two roommates, Eric, John, Kay, and Kevin.

The house in which they lived was organized in accordance with the guidelines of cooperative households. No power plays, no Rescues,*no lies, or secrets. Regular house meetings were held, and people committed themselves at the outset to submit to the concern and criticism of their housemates when things were not well. They agreed to be open to each other's feelings and paranoias, and if trouble developed, they agreed to engage in a mediation, a problem-solving process designed to deal with interpersonal difficulties. The house was owned by Clancy, but everyone shared the understanding that, except for her ultimate right to sell the house, with a minimum six months' notice, she would have no rights over and above anyone else's. She would get a fair amount of rent and then would be an equal among equals, sharing in the power and the decision making. After many questions and answers among all the participants, John, Mary, and the children were welcomed into the household and moved in.

John

Before John and Mary met, John had been strangely unhappy. After all, he was free from a very bad marriage,

* A Rescue is defined as a situation in which somebody either a). does what he doesn't want to do or b). does more than his share in a situation. A complete description of guidelines for cooperative living can be found in *Manual on Cooperation* written by myself.

had a good job, was making good money, had bought the new sporty car he had always wanted, had a nice bachelor apartment and a tender, considerate, undemanding lover. So why was he dissatisfied? It was not his style to ask himself searching questions, but had he done so he might have become aware that, even though he was working harder than he ever did before and earning more, he had less money and was more deeply in debt than he had ever been. He never actually sat down to make a budget but sensed that his medical insurance, high income taxes, together with gasoline, maintenance insurance and loan payments on his luxury car, frequent eating out, stylish clothes and skiing trips were consuming his relatively high income faster than it was produced. He had hoped eventually to own a home, but that was slowly becoming more and more unlikely. Most of his energies were devoted to his work, where he felt that he needed to make his mark before age forty. His job as a computer specialist at a successful electronics firm was highly stressful. The superficial, heady good spirits that prevailed at work just barely hid the competitive tension, the constant jockeying for position, and the clearly defined power ladder with its constant subtle power plays. After ten years of moderate success, he was tired of what increasingly felt like a rat race. He blamed himself; he lacked ambition, he wasn't a real competitor.

But none of these thoughts were really conscious to him. He knew only that he was strangely unhappy.

His relationship with Karla had suited his needs perfectly when they first met in the last year of his marriage. They had known each other at work and their distant working relationship became a sudden, passionate affair. Karla unlike John was satisfied with her marriage and liked her husband, who was aware of her relationship with John. John, weary of his own marriage, did not want a long term commitment, but needed the excitement of their relationship to have the strength to leave his wife. Karla and John's love affair became a sexual friendship which served them both well. They saw each other roughly every other week for intimate evening dates. They both liked to dance, went on little trips, and gave each other a great deal while demanding very little. John learned from Karla that a woman could be strong and self-sufficient. He learned to listen when she spoke of her feelings and he learned to speak of his own. They were very much alike, and liked and trusted each other.

Nevertheless, even this part of John's life seemed gray and lifeless lately. The way he put it to himself was that he either wanted more or less of Karla. As Woody Allen had put it: "A relationship is like a shark. It needs to keep moving or it dies." Things generally had not been moving. Meeting Mary had changed all that. At first he took his relationship to be a passing, albeit lovely, affair. Nowhere in his life-script was there a place for a serious commitment to a woman so different from him. Mary wore no make-up and could not wear high heels if her life depended on it, her clothes were strangely exotic (mostly culled from second-hand stores and reworked), and she ate peculiar food. She moved expansively and laughed broadly, her orgasms were cataclysmic, her car was a public embarrassment, and she refused to use birth-control pills. She was altogether different from the women he knew at work. He was fascinated by the fact that, unlike previous relationships in which the maximum attraction occurred first, the more he knew Mary the more he liked her. He was stunned by her honesty and constantly interested in her. He was able to adjust to the various shocking ideas which she occasionally uttered. "If I didn't ask for what I wanted, I would be lying." "Feelings are fact, paranoia is heightened awareness, intuition counts." "Science, technology, medical knowledge, milk, meat, and potatoes, and the American Dream are bankrupt." "We need a better idea and we better not expect Ford to come up with it." "Detonate the nuclear family."

"You know, Mary" he once said to her, "if anyone had told me a year ago that I would be moving into a cooperative house with a woman with two children, I would have said, 'You are crazy, better turn in your crystal ball; it needs an overhaul.'" To which Mary smiled slyly and responded, "If you think last year was amazing, wait till you see the next. I don't want you to call me crazy, so I won't tell. Fasten your safety belt."

John had a tendency to be sloppy in the kitchen and bathroom. This was unacceptable to the women in the house. He often did this when he was busy fixing the roof or doing the types of chores that men will do, but when he tried to point this out, Mary remarked that she would rather learn how to fix the roof than do his dirty dishes. At first he took this to be women's lib rhetoric but was surprised to find she meant it. Next time he climbed on the roof, she came along and he realized she could swing a hammer with the best. He found that teaching her his "manly" skills was a pleasure; she learned fast and was truly able to share in those chores which he had assumed were his exclusively. He learned to be neat in the kitchen. As they settled into their relationship, they were beginning to act like a married couple and experiencing a throwback to old patterns. They found themselves hiding their feelings sometimes, doing things they really did not want to do at other times; but because they had agreed to and because they truly wanted to, they continually struggled against these tendencies, talking about them, demanding complete honesty from each other, and being unwilling to tolerate power plays and Rescues when they saw them happen. They tried to be open to each other's criticism and made an effort to be open to the scrutiny and feedback of their housemates and friends. In these matters Mary tended to be the teacher, with John largely being the willing student.

As time passed John realized that his new relationship with Mary and the changes in his lifestyle were quickly becoming contradictory with the demands of his job. At work he was a cog in a strictly hierarchical machine. It was a good job, a job that taxed his creativity, and because of that he liked it. On the other hand the emotional vacuum that the job represented, the acquiescence to power plays and lies which was required of a person who worked there began to be a problem for him.

John's company, Lectrix, was quite successful and operated on the assumption that its success had something to do with the competitive, authoritarian structure of it. The employees at Lectrix were organized into what people liked to call a "family," though in truth it operated more like a professional football team. He began to see that the success of the company had to do more with a lucky combination of creative individuals and market conditions than with the way it was structured. In fact, it seemed to him that Lectrix was beginning to be harmed by some of the competitive assumptions within it. Several competing companies were challenging Lectrix, and the lack of warmth and trust at work was creating stress, absenteeism, and sickness. He sensed that he could not abide the contradictions between his private and work life much longer. He resolved to either change the environment at work or to change jobs. Because he was a rather senior member and because he was respected by his colleagues, he had faith that he would be heard when he proposed some of the changes that he had in mind. He gave himself a year to accomplish these changes, after which if he had no success he would look for employment elsewhere or possibly start his own company in which democratic management, cooperation, and honesty were an integral part of the functioning. He had gained the confidence that this was possible because he had observed Mary at her workplace, a collectively owned bookstore which was successful in the field and operated according to cooperative norms and aspirations, organized on non-hierarchical lines. He was excited by the prospect of making his workplace an enjoyable part of his life in which he felt involved and powerful.

One evening when John came home from work, he and Mary had a sudden, unpleasant interaction. They had been gently disagreeing over the last weeks about what John's responsibilities were with respect to the care of Mary's children. But this evening, with John and Mary both exhausted from work, their disagreement flared up into open warfare.

John had agreed to share with Mary in child care; just how much had not been made clear. Frequently, recently, he fell short of her expectations. When he got home and she asked him to spend some time with Kay, he ignored her, pretending not to hear.

"Did you hear me ask you to watch Kay?"

"Yes."

"Why didn't you answer?"

"I don't know. I didn't feel like it."

"Well that's a hell of a reason!"

"It's as good a reason as I need."

"What do you mean by that?"

"I don't *have* to take care of Kay, do I?"

"Well, that's interesting. What else don't you have to do? Do you have to fuck me? And if you do, do you have to keep it up?"

John looked at her stunned. He was about to come back with a whopper when Mary said, "I'm sorry, that wasn't fair. We have to talk this over calmly."

But John was hurt. He realized that recently their sexual life, so wonderful at first, was becoming somewhat routine. It began to happen oftener than not that Mary was eager to have sex and John preferred not to. At first this was not a problem because John truly enjoyed sex with Mary, but a couple of times he had gone along when he really was not interested. He began to become aware of his unexpected lack of interest, and he had not spoken freely about it, thereby violating his cooperative agreements with Mary. Mary began to notice and asked whether there might be something wrong. John denied it, knowing at the very moment that he did that he was making a big mistake. She accepted his denial, but his feelings continued and she continued to be attuned to them and at times she became seriously concerned that she was no longer attractive to him, that he no longer loved her. Until that point Mary hadn't minded John's relationship with Karla, but now she became secretly angry and she began to notice other slights and other small hurtful incidents. One thing in particular, even though no clean-cut agreement had been made about it, was the continuing shortfall in John's child care. Now she was openly angry and realized that the situation needed some close attention.

John and Mary agreed that they needed a mediation.* Mary contacted her group's facilitator, who recommended one of her colleagues because John felt that he preferred to work with somebody who knew them both equally well. A date was set with Michael, who asked them to come to the meeting prepared to share any feelings that they had not expressed, any Rescues that they had engaged in, and any paranoid fantasies that they had about each other.

They met in the evening after work at Michael's home. After some small talk, Michael began:

"Let's start by checking in and exchanging feelings, paranoid fantasies, and Rescues. Who wants to jump in?"

John volunteered; "I have something. Okay, Mary?"

Mary nodded nervously.

"Mary," said John, "I feel you were very unfair to me the other day and it made me feel bad."

Michael interrupted. "Hold on, let's get this straight; what did Mary do and what did you feel? When you say that you feel Mary was very unfair, you are not telling us a feeling, you are giving us an opinion about her behavior. What did you feel? Feeling bad isn't really clear. What exactly was the feeling?"

John thought about it. "I felt angry."

"Did you feel something else?"

"Actually at first I felt hurt and sad. Then I got furious."

"Okay, now we know how you felt. When did you feel this? What did Mary do to cause you to feel that way?"

John turned to Mary.

"Mary, when you said those things to me on Tuesday, after work, I was very hurt and angry."

* See *Solving Problems Together* by Hogie Wyckoff and *A Manual on Mediation* by Becky Jenkins and Claude Steiner for details on the process of mediation.

Mary nodded quietly. After a brief silence, she answered. "I have a paranoid fantasy for you; do you want to hear it?"

John nodded his head. "Yes."

Mary took a deep breath and said, "John, I am afraid that you are lying to me about our relationship and that you are turned off to me and that you like Karla more than you like me."

John sat back thoughtfully. After some time he said:

"No, Mary, I am not turned off to you. Really—and I don't prefer Karla to you, either. The grain of truth in your suspicions is that I did lie to you when you asked me whether there was something wrong a couple of weeks ago, because I should have told you then what I want to tell you now. It has to do with our sex. Do you want to hear?"

"Yes," said Mary. "Please." Then she took a big breath, looked at Michael, and said, "I'm scared."

Michael eyed her with concern. "Are you okay? Do you need something?"

"I'm okay. Go ahead, John, I want to hear."

"Well, Mary, I'm not sure what is going on, but recently I have been worried because sometimes, in the middle of sex, I get turned off and I begin to lose my erection, and that really scares me. That's why I sometimes don't want to have sex—because I am afraid that that will happen."

Michael asked: "Why do you think you get turned off? Is it something Mary does?"

"Well, I don't know; she gets so lost in sex and it bothers me for some reason."

Mary flared up, "Is there something wrong with that? Do I get too excited for you?"

Michael interceded. "Relax, Mary; don't jump to conclusions." Turning to John he asked, "Why do you think that you get turned off?"

"I don't know."

"Think about it. Why?"

John thought for a long while. "I think I am afraid that she'll get pregnant. I know how Mary feels about having an abortion and how upsetting the abortion she had years ago was, how sad it made her, and I don't want to be involved in that. When I start thinking about her getting pregnant, I can't stop thinking about it and I get turned off. I don't know; it's all very confusing. The only time that I feel okay about sex is when Mary is having her period and I am pretty sure she won't get pregnant."

Mary started crying. After a while she looked up and she said:

"I'm so relieved that is what is going on. I have been having similar thoughts. I don't want to get pregnant either. I love you, John; I don't care whether you fuck me or not." Through her tears she looked at John and, with a smile, said, "Well, that's a little strong. You know what I mean. What are we going to do?"

The mediation went on for two hours in which John and Mary shared further feelings about child care, about Karla, about their commitment.

As they exchanged their feelings, the problem became clear. John and Mary's commitment was deepening. Neither of them wanted any more children. A vasectomy for John became a real strong possibility as a means of taking care of their sexual problem. He had been contemplating that alternative for some years and the time seemed ripe.

John was earnestly committed to sharing child care with Mary, but not quite on a half-and-half basis, so they settled on one third. About Karla, Mary felt that she was a good friend of John's and she did not want to interfere. She sometimes got jealous, but with a little extra attention from John, she knew it would be no real problem. She enjoyed the time she spent without John on the occasional evenings of his dates with Karla and did not want to change that for the sake of dealing with the occasional jealous twinge it caused her. It gave her a feeling of freedom and independence to know that both she and John gave each other the choice of having other close friends. She did ask that if their relationship remained problematic that he would consider not having sex with Karla. He readily agreed, though he worried about how Karla would feel about that. He decided to discuss it with her.

The mediation ended with Mary and John hugging each other and feeling great tenderness and love for each other. After giving Michael strokes for a job well done, they went out for a lobster dinner to celebrate how they felt.

The mediation worked. John got a vasectomy and did his child care religiously; actually he enjoyed the children a lot. Their sex life straightened right out. Eventually John quit his job and became a consultant for electronic firms. He took a salary cut, but his expenses had been trimmed and he enjoyed his independence. In his spare time, he worked on an old apartment house he and Mary and several others bought as a cooperative condominium and turned it into a cooperative household like Clancy's, only with separate apartments and one of the apartments remodelled into one large common kitchen. After years of being together, John and Mary marvelled at how well they got along. Sometimes it seemed that they would live happily (well, almost; it wasn't always perfect) ever after.

BIBLIOGRAPHY

1. Americans for Democratic Action, *A Citizen's Guide to the Right Wing*. 1411 K Street N.W., Washington, D.C., 1978.
2. Berne, Eric, *Beyond Games and Scripts*. New York: Grove Press, 1976.
3. ———, *Games People Play*. New York: Grove Press, 1964.
4. ———, *Transactional Analysis in Psychotherapy*. New York: Grove Press, 1961.
5. Caro, Robert A., *The Power Broker*. New York: Knopf, 1974.
6. Castaneda, Carlos, *A Separate Reality*. New York: Simon and Schuster, 1971.
7. ———, *Tales of Power*. New York: Touchstone, 1976.
8. Cooker, Virginia, and others, *Resource Manual for a Living Revolution*. Philadelphia: Movement New Society, 1978.
9. Craig, James H. and Marguerite, *Synergic Power*. Berkeley: Proactive Press, 1974.
10. Domhoff, G. William, *The Bohemian Grove and Other Retreats*. New York: Harper and Row, 1975.
11. Dyer, Wayne, *Pulling Your Own Strings*. New York: Avon Books, 1979.
12. Freundlich, Paul, and others, *Guide to Cooperative Alternatives*. Louisa, Virginia: Community Publications Cooperative, 1979.
13. Friedman, Mayer, and Pusenman, Ray, *Type A Behavior and Your Heart*. New York: Fawcett, 1978.
14. Haley, Jay, *The Power Tactics of Jesus Christ and Other Essays*. New York: Avon Books, 1969.

15. Haragan, Betty, *Games Mother Never Taught You.* New York: Warner Books, 1978.
16. Henley, Nancy, *Body Politics.* New Jersey: Prentice-Hall, 1977.
17. Hitler, Adolph, *Mein Kampf.* Boston: Houghton Mifflin, 1962.
18. Hutschnecker, Arnold, *The Drive for Power.* New York: M. Evans, 1974.
19. Jenkins, Becky, and Steiner, Claude, *Mediations.* Berkeley: I.R.T. Press, Box 5039, Berkeley, CA 94705, 1980.
20. Kerr, Carmen, *Sex for Women.* New York: Grove Press, 1977.
21. Korda, Michael, *Male Chauvinism!* New York: Random House, 1973.
22. ———, *Power!* New York: Random House, 1975.
23. ———, "Psychodynamics of Power," *Mainliner,* March, 1977.
24. ———, *Success!* New York: Random House, 1977.
25. Kropotkin, Peter, *Mutual Aid.* Boston: Extending Horizon Books, 1976, reproduction of 1904 edition.
26. Laing, Ronald D., *The Politics of the Family.* New York: Pantheon Books, 1971.
27. Lerner, Michael, "Surplus Powerlessness," *Social Policy,* February, 1979.
28. Machiavelli, Nicolo, *The Prince.* New York: Dutton, 1958.
29. May, Rollo, *Power and Innocence.* New York: W. W. Norton, 1972.
30. McClelland, David, *Power: The Inner Experience.* New York: Irvington Publishers, 1975.
31. Milgram, Stanley, *Obedience to Authority.* New York: Harper and Row, 1974.
32. Mintz, Morton, and Cohen, Jerry S., *America, Inc., Who Owns and Operates the United States.* New York: Dial, 1971.
33. ———, *Power, Inc.* New York: Bantam, 1977.
34. Morrisson, R.H., *Why Sons of Bitches Succeed and Why Nice Guys Fail in Small Business.* New York: S.M.A. Publishers, 1973.
35. Newfield, Jack, and Du Brul, Paul, *The Abuse of Power.* New York: Viking, 1977.
36. Newman, Mildred, and Berkowitz, Bernard, *How to be Your Own Best Friend.* New York: Ballantine, 1974.

37. Ringer, Robert, *Looking Out for No. 1*. New York: Fawcett, 1977.

38. ———, *Restoring the American Dream*. New York: Fawcett, 1979.

39. ———, *Winning Through Intimidation*. New York: Fawcett, 1974.

40. Rogers, Carl, *On Personal Power*. New York: Delacorte Press, 1977.

41. Rosenberg, Marshall, *From Now On*. St. Louis: Community Psychological Consultants, 1740 Gulf Drive, St. Louis, MO 63130, 1979.

42. Schwebel, Robert, "Blaming Yourself and Shared Responsibility," *Issues in Cooperative Power*, 1:4, Winter, 1980.

43. Smith, Manuel J., *When I Say No I Feel Guilty*. New York: Dial, 1975.

44. Steiner, Claude, *Feminism for Men*. Berkeley: I.R.T. Press, n.d.

45. ———, *Healing Alcoholism*. New York: Grove Press, 1980.

46. ———, *Manual on Cooperation*. Berkeley: I.R.T. Press, n.d.

47. ———, *Scripts People Live*. New York: Grove Press, 1974.

48. ———, "Radical Psychiatry Manifesto," in Claude Steiner, ed., *Readings in Radical Psychiatry*. New York: Grove Press, 1974.

49. Wyckoff, Hogie, *Solving Problems Together*. New York: Grove Press, 1980.

50. Wikse, John R., *About Possession: The Self as Private Property*. University Park and London: Pennsylvania State University Press, 1977.